Book of Classic Knitting Patterns

Book of
Classic Knitting Patterns

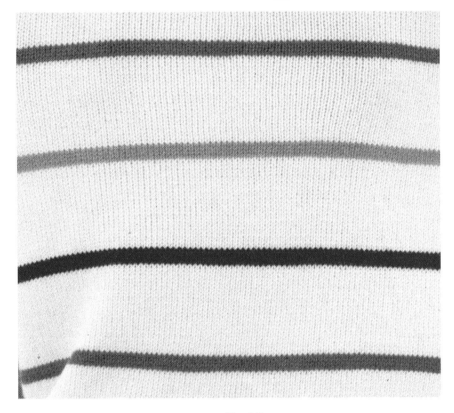

compiled by
PHILLIPA DAVIS

NEW
HOLLAND

New Holland (Publishers) Ltd
37 Connaught Street, London W2 2AZ

First published in the UK in 1989

ISBN 1 85368 018 4

Designed by Joan Sutton
Lithographic reproduction by Unifoto (Pty) Ltd
Typeset by McManus Bros (Pty) Ltd
Printed and bound by CTP Book Printers

Contents

Introduction

Knitting is a pastime that brings not only pleasure, but profit and a tremendous sense of accomplishment. An idea initially conceived in early Egypt and further developed by the fishermen of the biblical era, knitting has become part of our heritage.

The yarns available today provide the knitter with a versatile product that covers all requirements in colour range, quality, washability and long lasting wear. The patterns in the *Pingouin Book of Classic Knitting Patterns* have been designed by Pingouin to give you a choice of basic knits, interesting Fair Isles and fashion knits for the whole family.

Pingouin yarns and Inox needles were used in making the garments in this book, but if for any reason they are unavailable, your local wool shop will be able to recommend suitable alternative yarns and needles. If you do use yarn other than that recommended, it is even more imperative to knit a test square to check your tension. We trust that you will enjoy making up the garments in this book during your well-deserved hours of relaxation.

Patterns

The first row after casting on is usually regarded as the right side of the work. The first row of any pattern is the right side unless otherwise stated. Stitches given between * and * should be repeated across the row ending as indicated. Stitches inside square brackets [ ] must be worked the number of times stated, e.g. [K2tog, K1] 7 times. Number of stitches that should be on needles is indicated in [ ] at various points in the pattern.

Sizes

Where garments are in more than one size the smallest size is given first with any necessary alterations for the larger sizes given in round brackets ( ) in size order. If there is only one figure it applies to all sizes.

Tension

Before beginning work, it is essential to knit a tension square. Unless otherwise stated on the pattern, it should be in stocking stitch. Cast on the number of stitches required for 10 cm and work the number of rows stated for 10 cm. To measure the square, lay it on a flat surface without stretching (do not use your lap). If your square is slightly more than 10 cm, use a smaller needle; if slightly less than 10 cm, use a larger needle. Remember that a 6 mm smaller square would result in a garment 6 cm smaller, and a 6 mm larger square would make it 6 cm larger on a 91 cm bust size.

The extra time spent in the beginning on a tension square means the difference between a garment that does not fit and one that fits perfectly.

ABBREVIATIONS

alt	–	alternate		
beg	–	begin(ning)		
CC	–	contrast colour		
ch	–	chain		
cm(s)	–	centimetre(s)		
CN	–	cable needle		
c/on (off)	–	cast on (off)		
cont	–	continue		
dc	–	double crochet		
d inc	–	double increase, P into front, K into back, then P into front of same stitch		
dec	–	decrease		
fol	–	following		
gst	–	garter stitch; knit every row		
IM	–	Irish Moss stitch		
inc(s)	–	increase(s)		
K	–	knit		
kfb	–	knit into front and back of stitch		
K1 below	–	knit into next stitch one row below, at the same time dropping off stitch above		
K(P)W	–	knit (purl) wise		
lp(s)	–	loop(s)		
MC	–	main colour		
m1	–	make one stitch, pick up loop and knit (purl) into back		
mst	–	moss stitch		
N(s)	–	needle(s)		

P	–	purl
patt(s)	–	pattern(s)
psso	–	pass slipped stitch over
rem	–	remain(ing)
rep	–	repeat
rev	–	reverse
rev st st	–	reverse stocking stitch, purlside as right side
R(L)HS	–	right (left) hand side
RW	–	ribwise
R(W)S	–	right (wrong) side
SKPO	–	slip one, knit one, pass slipped stitch over
SKTPO	–	slip one, knit two together, pass slipped stitch over
sl	–	slip
st(s)	–	stitch(es)
st st	–	stocking stitch (1 row K, 1 row P)
tbl	–	through back of loop
tog	–	together
tr	–	treble crochet
V	–	lengthen or shorten here
yb	–	yarn back
yfd	–	yarn forward
yon	–	yarn over needle
yrn	–	yarn round needle

Special abbreviations

C4B or C4F – Cable 4 back or front – Slip next 2 stitches onto cable needle and hold at back (or front) of work, knit next 2 stitches from lefthand needle, then knit stitches from cable needle.

It is inadvisable to experiment with a different stitch from that shown on the pattern. You need more yarn and more stitches for a ribbed or cabled garment than you do for a garment in stocking stitch.

Buttonholes

These are usually worked by casting off a number of stitches. On the following row complete the buttonhole by casting on the same number of stitches over those cast off on the previous row. When buttonholes are worked in a vertical border always measure from the **cast-off** edge of the previous one.

Make up

Unless otherwise stated, use a fine back-stitch for the side and sleeve seams and a flat stitch for welts.

Basic stitches

All special stitches are fully described in the patterns to which they apply. For ready reference and the less experienced knitter, however, all the basic stitches are set out below. All abbreviations as well as needle conversion tables and international yarn label symbols are fully explained opposite.

Knitting

Single rib (even number of sts) – **Every row:** * K1, P1; rep from * to end. (odd number of sts) – **First row:** K1, * P1, K1; rep from * to end. **2nd row:** P1, * K1, P1; rep from * to end. Rep these 2 rows.
Double rib (worked on a multiple of 4 sts) – **Every row:** * K2, P2; rep from * to end. Double rib is often arranged so that right-side rows beg and end K2 and wrong-side rows P2.
Stocking stitch – **First row** (right side): K. **2nd row:** P.
Reversed stocking stitch – **First row** (right side): P. **2nd row:** K.
Garter stitch – every row: K.
Moss stitch – **First row:** * K1, P1; rep from * to end. **2nd row:** K the P sts and P the K sts.

Crochet

Chain – Beg with a loop already on hook, pass hook under the yarn and draw a loop through.
Slip-sts – Insert hook under the chain or into a stitch in previous row, yarn over hook and draw it through the stitch of chain and through the chain already on hook.
Double crochet – Insert hook under a chain or into a stitch in previous row; yarn over hook, draw a loop through, yarn over hook and draw through the 2 loops on hook.
Treble – Yarn over hook, insert hook under a chain or into a stitch in previous row, yarn over hook and draw a loop through, yarn over hook and draw it through 2 loops, yarn over hook and draw through remaining 2 loops.

NEEDLECHART

OLD GAUGE (English)	NEW GAUGE (in mm)	US GAUGE
000	10	15
00	9	13
0	8	12
1	7,5	11
2	7	10½
3	6,5	10
4	6	9
5	5,5	8
6	5	7
7	4,5	6
8	4	5
9	3,75	4
10	3,25	3
11	3	2
12	2,75	1
13	2,25	1
14	2	00

CROCHET

OLD GAUGE (English)	NEW GAUGE (in mm)	US GAUGE
2	7	K/10
4	6	J/10
5	5,5	I/9
6	5	H/8
7	4,5	G/6
8	4	F/5
9	3,5	E/4
10	3	D/3
12	2,5	C/2
14	2	B/1
15	1,75	6
16	1,5	7

Age	8 years	10 years	12 years	14 years
Height (in cms)	126	138	150	160
Chest	64	70	76	82
Waist	58	60	62	65
Hip	70	76	82	88
Back waist length	30	32	35	39
Arm length	45	50	54	58

The measurements quoted on the chart refer to actual body measurements and not to finished measurements.
Select pattern size, allowances being made to insure a proper fit.

YARN LABEL SYMBOLS

NEEDLES, HOOK AND METERAGE	
METRIC 3,75 – 4 ENGLISH 8 – 9	Manufacturer's suggested knitting needle size with metric and English sizes. **Note:** The pattern you select for the yarn may call for a needle size smaller or larger than the recommended size given. Use the recommended needle size for the pattern when determining your gauge.
METRIC 3 ENGLISH 10	Manufacturer's suggested crochet hook size. See note under knitting needles.
200 m	Meterage per ball
WASHING	
	Note: The washing symbols used by yarn companies vary. Some yarns labelled with just the tub and temperature are not always machine washable. Always take care when attempting to wash any yarn by machine that is not specifically called 'machine washable.'
MACHINE	
40°C WOOL CYCLE	machine washable at stated temperature – wool cycle
40°C	machine washable at stated temperature **Note:** 40 °C = approximately 100 °F
HAND	
40°C	hand washable at temperature stated

BLEACHING	
	NO BLEACHING
PRESSING	
	DO NOT PRESS
	press with a cool iron
	press with a warm iron
	press with a hot iron
DRY CLEANING	
(F)	may be dry cleaned with fluorocarbon or petroleum based solvents only
(P)	may be dry cleaned with perchlorethylene or fluorocarbon or petroleum based solvents
(A)	may be dry cleaned with all solutions
	Note: It may be necessary to ask your dry cleaner which solutions are used to clean your knitwear.
MISCELLANEOUS SYMBOLS	
	suitable for machine knitting
10	needs 10 balls of yarn for average sweater

Swiss Darning

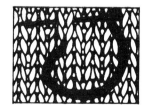 

Bring needle up through centre of stitch from back of work, insert from right to left behind stitch immediately above (see diagram 1), then down through centre of original stitch and out through centre of next stitch to left. (See diagram 2). Proceed in this manner in horizontal rows from right to left or vice versa.

Baby's sweaters and cardigans

MATERIALS
Corrida 4 (50 g balls), 4(5;5) balls per item. One pair each 3,25 mm and 4 mm knitting needles; 3 mm crochet hook; 3 buttons for sweaters; 4 buttons for cardigans.

MEASUREMENTS
To fit chest 40 (45;50) cm.

TENSION
22 sts and 30 rows = 10 cm square measured over st st using 4 mm Ns.

BACK (for all styles)
Using 3,25 mm Ns c/on 51(57;63) sts.
First row (right side): K1, *P1, K1; rep from * to end.
2nd row: P1, *K1, P1; rep from * to end.
Rep the last 2 rows 4 times more★.
Change to 4 mm Ns and work in st st, until back measures 12(14;16) cms or required length to armholes ending with a P row.

SHAPE RAGLAN ARMHOLES
C/off 2(3;3) sts at beg of next 2 rows.
3rd row: K1, sl 1, K1, psso, K to last 3 sts, K2tog, K1.
4th row: P.★★
Rep the last 2 rows until 21(21;23) sts rem ending with the P row.
Next row: K1, sl 1, K2tog, psso, K to last 4 sts, K3tog, K1.
Next row: P.
Slip rem 17(17;19) sts onto a holder for Sweater, c/off for Cardigan.

SLEEVES (for all styles)
Using 3,25 mm Ns c/on 31(33;35) sts and work 10 rows in K1, P1 rib as given for Back. Change to 4 mm Ns and work 4 rows in st st, starting K. Inc 1 st at each end of next and every fol 4th (5th;6th) row until there are 41(43;47) sts. Work straight until sleeve measures 13(15;17) cms or required seam length ending with a P row.

SHAPE RAGLAN TOP
C/off 2(3;3) sts at beg of next 2 rows. Work 2 rows straight.
Next row: K1, sl 1, K1, psso, K to last 3 sts, K2tog, K1.
Next row: P.
2nd and 3rd sizes only: Rep last 4 rows twice more.
All sizes: Rep the last 2 rows only until 15 sts rem ending with the P row.
Next row: K1, sl 1, K2tog, psso, K to last 4 sts, K3tog, K1.
Next row: P.
Rep last 2 rows once more. Slip rem 7 sts onto a holder for Sweater, c/off for Cardigan.

Patterned front sweater
Work as given for Back to ★. Change to 4 mm Ns and commence pattern panel:-
First row: K13(16;18), P1, C4B, K2 [P1, K1] 5(5;6) times, P1, C4B, K2, P1, K to end.
2nd row: P13(16;18), K1, P6, [K1, P1] 5(5;6) times, K1, P6, K1, P to end.
3rd row: K13(16;18), P1, K2, C4F, P11(11;13), K2, C4F, P1, K to end.
4th row: P13(16;18), K1, P6, K11(11;13), P6, K1, P to end.
The last 4 rows form the pattern. Keeping pattern correct work straight until front measures same as back to armhole ending with a WS row.

SHAPE RAGLAN ARMHOLES
Keeping pattern correct c/off 2(3;3) sts at beg of next 2 rows.
3rd row: K1, sl 1, K1, psso, work in patt to last 3 sts, K2tog, K1.
4th row: P2, work in patt to last 2 sts, P2.
Keeping pattern correct complete as given for Plain Front Sweater from ★★★ to end.

MAKE UP AND NECKBAND
Join front raglan seams and right back raglan seam.
Neckband: Using 3,25 mm Ns and with RS of work facing, K across sts on holder at left sleeve top, pick up and K8(10;10) sts down left front slope, K across sts on holder at front neck, pick up and K8(10;10) sts up right front slope, then K across sts on holders at right sleeve top and back neck inc 1 st at centre back.
First row: P1, *K1, P1; rep from * to end.
Work 5 more rows in rib. C/off loosely in rib.

Join side and sleeve seams. Join rem raglan seam leaving 8 cm open at top. Using crochet hook work 1 row of double crochet round opening, then work a 2nd row making 3 buttonloops evenly spaced on one side. Press seams. Sew on buttons.

Plain cardigan

LEFT FRONT
Using 3,25 mm Ns c/on 28(32;34) sts.
First row (right side): * K1, P1; rep from * to last 6 sts, K6.
2nd row: K5, P1, * K1, P1; rep from * to end.

Rep the last 2 rows 4 times more, inc 1 st at end of last row. [29(33;35) sts.]
★ Change to 4 mm Ns and keeping gst border correct, work in st st starting K until front measures same as back to armholes ending at side edge.

SHAPE RAGLAN ARMHOLE AND FRONT NECK
C/off 2(3;3) sts at beg of next row.
2nd row: K5, P to end.
3rd row: K1, sl 1, K1, psso, K to last 7 sts, K2tog, K5.
Dec 1 st at raglan edge as before on every alt row, **at the same time** dec 1 st inside gst border as before on every alt row twice more, then every fol 4th row 4(5;5) times. [9(9;11) sts rem.] Keeping neck edge straight cont raglan decs on every alt row as before until 7 sts rem.
★★ **Next row:** K5, P2tog tbl.
Next row: K2tog, K4. [5 sts rem.]
Work 20(20;22) rows in gst on rem 5 sts. C/off.

Mark positions on front for 4 buttons, the first to be on 5th row of welt and the 4th to be 1 cm below first neck dec. Space rem 2 evenly between.

RIGHT FRONT

Using 3,25 mm Ns c/on 28(32;34) sts.
First row: K6, * P1, K1; rep from * to end.
2nd row: * P1, K1; rep from * to last 6 sts, P1, K5.
Rep the last 2 rows once more.
Next row (buttonhole): K1, K2tog, yf, K3, * P1, K1; rep from * to end.
Work 5 more rows in gst and rib inc 1 st at beg of last row. [29(33;35) sts.]
★★★
Change to 4 mm Ns and keeping gst border correct and making buttonholes to match markers on RS rows as before, work in st st until front measures same as back to armholes ending at side edge.

SHAPE RAGLAN ARMHOLE AND FRONT NECK

C/off 2(3;3) sts at beg of next row.
Next row: K5, sl 1, K1, psso, K to last 3 sts, K2tog, K1. Complete to match left front rev shapings.

Plain front sweater

Work as given for Back to ★★.
★★★ Rep the last two rows until 27(29;31) sts rem ending with the dec row.

SHAPE FRONT NECK

Next row: Work 9(10;10) sts, turn and complete this side first.
Cont to dec at raglan edge as before on next and every alt row, **at the same time** dec 1 st at neck edge on next 3 rows. Keeping neck edge straight cont raglan decs only until 3 sts rem. Dec 1 st at neck edge only on fol alt row. C/off.

Slip centre 9(9;11) sts onto a holder for neckband. With WS of work facing re-join yarn to neck edge of rem sts and work to end. Complete to match first side rev shapings.

Patterned cardigan

LEFT FRONT

Work as given for left front of Plain Cardigan to ★. Change to 4 mm Ns and commence patt:–
First row: [P1, K1] 8(10;11) times, P1, C4B, K2, P1, K5.
2nd row: K6, P6, K1, [P1, K1] 8(10;11) times.
3rd row: P17(21;23), K2, C4F, P1, K5.
4th row: K6, P6, K to end.
The last 4 rows form the pattern. Keeping gst border and pattern correct work straight until front measures same as back to armholes ending at side edge.

SHAPE RAGLAN ARMHOLE AND FRONT NECK

Keeping patt correct c/off 2(3;3) sts at beg of next row.
Next row: K5, work in patt to last 2 sts, P2.
Next row: K1, sl 1, K1, psso, work to last 14 sts, P2tog, work in patt to end.

Rep the last 2 rows twice more. [21(24;26) sts rem.] Continue to dec at raglan edge on every alt row as before, **at the same time** dec 1 st inside border on every fol 4th row until 15(15;17) sts rem ending with the dec row.
Next row: Work to last 2 sts, P2.
Next row: K1, sl 1, K1, psso, work to end.
Next row: Work to last 2 sts, P2.
Next row: K1, sl 1, K2tog, psso, work to end.
Rep the last 4 rows once more. [9(9;11) sts rem.] Dec 1 st at raglan edge as before on every alt row until 7 sts rem.

Complete as given for left front of Plain Cardigan from ★★ to end.

RIGHT FRONT

Work as given for right front of Plain Cardigan to ★★★. Change to 4 mm Ns and commence patt:–
First row: K5, P1, C4B, K2, P1, [K1, P1] 8(10;11) times.
2nd row: [K1, P1] 8(10;11) times, K1, P6, K6.
3rd row: K5, P1, K2, C4F, P17(21;23).
4th row: K17(21;23), P6, K6.
Keeping gst border and pattern correct and making buttonholes to match markers on RS rows as before, work straight until front measures same as back to armholes ending at side edge.

SHAPE RAGLAN ARMHOLE AND FRONT NECK

Keeping patt correct c/off 2(3;3) sts at beg of next row.
Next row: Work 12 sts, P2tog, work to last 3 sts, K2tog, K1.
Complete to match left front reversing shaping.

TO MAKE UP

Join raglan, side and sleeve seams. Join ends of neckband and sew in place across back neck. Press seams. Sew on buttons.

Baby layette in yellow

MATERIALS

France + (50 g balls); 6(7;8) balls. One pair each 3 mm, 3,25 mm and 4 mm knitting needles; 7 buttons; 2 stitch holders.

MEASUREMENTS

To fit chest 47(51;56) cm; side seam 15(17;19) cm; leg seam 21(23;25) cm; sleeve length 17(17;19) cm.

TENSION

24 sts and 33 rows = 10 cm over st st using 3,25 mm Ns.
25 sts and 34 rows = 10 cm over patt st using 4 mm Ns.

Cardigan

Worked in one piece to underarm.
Using 3 mm Ns, c/on 125(135;145) sts and work 1,5 cm in K1, P1 rib. Change to 4 mm Ns and patt as follows:
First row: P1(6;1) * K3, P7; rep from * to last 4(9;4) sts, K3, P1(6;1).
2nd and 3rd rows: K the K sts and P the P sts.
4th row: P to end.
5th row: P6(1;6), * K3, P7; rep from * to last 9(4;9) sts, K3, P6(1;6).
6th and 7th rows: As 2nd and 3rd.
8th row: P to end.
These 8 rows form the patt. Cont in patt until work measures 15(17;19) cm from beg, ending with a WS row.

SHAPE ARMHOLES

Patt 27(29;31), c/off 8(9;10) sts for armhole, patt 55(59;63), c/off 8(9;10) sts for 2nd armhole, patt 27(29;31) sts. Cont in patt on these sts for left front only, until work measures 23(25;28) cm from beg, ending with a RS row.

SHAPE NECK

C/off at beg of next and every fol alt row as follows:
4(5;6) sts (once), 3 sts (once), 2 sts (once) and 1 st (twice). Cont in patt un-

til work measures 27(29;32) cm from beg, ending with a WS row.

SHAPE SHOULDER
C/off 8(8;9) sts at beg of next row and 8(9;9) sts on fol alt row. Rejoin yarn to armhole of right front, and complete to match left front, rev shapings.

BACK
With WS facing, rejoin yarn to rem sts and cont in patt until work measures 27(29;32) cm from beg.

SHAPE SHOULDERS
C/off 8(8;9) sts at beg of next 2 rows and 8(9;9) sts at beg of fol 2 rows. C/off rem 23(25;27) sts.

SLEEVE
Using 3 mm Ns, c/on 50(50;54) sts and work 1,5 cm in K1, P1 rib. Change to 4 mm Ns and patt.
First and **2nd size** beg * K3, P7; rep from * to end.
3rd size beg P2 * K3, P7; rep from * to last 2 sts, K2.
Keeping patt correct inc 1 st each end of every 10th row 4 times. [58(58;62) sts.] Cont in patt until work measures 17(17;19) cm from beg. C/off.

TO MAKE UP
Stitch shoulder and sleeve seams. Set sleeves in and stitch into position.

BUTTONHOLE BAND
With RS facing and using 3 mm Ns, pick up and K approximately 70(74;78) sts along front edge. Work 4 rows K1, P1 rib, working 4 buttonholes (2 sts wide) on 2nd row, the first 5 sts in from lower edge and the others 14(15;16) sts apart. C/off RW.

BUTTON BAND
Work as for buttonhole band, omitting buttonholes.

NECKBAND
With RS facing, using 3 mm Ns, pick up and K approximately 59(63;67) sts around neck. Work 4 rows K1, P1 rib, working a buttonhole on 2nd row, 2 sts in from edge. C/off. Sew on buttons.

Dungarees
RIGHT LEG
Using 3 mm Ns, c/on 46(50;54) sts and work 3 cm in K1, P1 rib. Change to 3,25 mm Ns and working in st st, inc 12 sts evenly across first row. Cont

straight on 58(62;66) sts until work measures 17(19;21) cm from beg, ending with a WS row. Inc 1 st each end of next and every fol 4th row 3 times in all. Cont straight on 64(68;72) sts until work measures 21(23;25) cm from beg, ending with a WS row. Leave on a spare N.

LEFT LEG
Work as for right leg. K across left leg and across right leg sts. P 1 row across 128(136;144) sts. Dec 1 st each end and 2 sts at centre = (SKTPO) on next and fol 2 alt rows. Cont straight on rem 116(124;132) sts until work measures 34(38;42) cm from beg ending with a WS row. Change to 3 mm Ns and work 1,5 cm K1, P1 rib. Change back to 3,25 mm Ns and st st until work measures 40(45;49) cm from beg ending with a RS row.

DIVIDE FOR ARMHOLES
P24(26;27), c/off 7(8;10) sts, P 54(56;58), c/off 7(8;10) sts, P rem 24(26;27) sts for left back. K 1 row across these sts.

SHAPE ARMHOLE
C/off 1 st at beg of next and fol 2 alt rows. Cont straight on rem 21(23;24) sts until work measures 44(49;53) cm from beg, ending with a WS row.

SHAPE BACK NECK
C/off 4(4;5) sts at beg of next row, 3 sts at beg of fol alt row, 2 sts at beg of fol 1(2;2) alt rows and 1 st on fol 2 alt rows. Cont straight on rem 10 sts until work measures 23(25;27) cm from last row of waist rib, ending with a WS row.
Next row (buttonhole): K2tog, K2, c/off 2, K2, K2tog.
Next row: P, c/on 2 sts over c/off sts.
Dec 1 st each end of next row. P 1 row. C/off.

FRONT
With RS facing, rejoin yarn to rem sts.

SHAPE ARMHOLES
C/off 1 st each end of next and fol 2 alt rows. Cont straight on rem 48(50;52) sts until work measures 42(47;51) cm from beg, ending with a WS row.

SHAPE NECK
K16, c/off 16(18;20) sts, K to end. Cont each side separately. C/off at neck edge on alt rows as follows:
2 sts (twice) and 1 st (twice). Cont straight on rem 10 sts until work measures 19(21;23) cm, from last row of

waist rib. Dec 1 st each end of next and fol alt row. C/off. Rejoin yarn to right back and complete to match left back rev shapings.

TO MAKE UP
Stitch leg seams and back seam.

BORDERS
Back: with RS facing and using 3 mm Ns pick up and K sts evenly along one edge of armhole strap, around neck and one side of 2nd armhole. Work 2 rows K1, P1 rib. C/off.
Front: work as for back. Sew on buttons.

Bootees

Using 3 mm Ns, c/on 36(38;42) sts and work 3 cm in K1, P1 rib. Change to 3,25 mm Ns and cont in st st until work measures 9(10;11) cm from beg. Place 12(12;14) sts at each end of work on a st holder. Cont straight on rem 12(14;14) sts for a further 4(4;5;5) cm. Break yarn. With RS facing K across 12 (12;14) sts on st holder, pick up and K 14(14;16) sts along instep, K across centre 12(14;14) sts, pick up and K14(14;16) sts along 2nd side of instep. K across 12(12;14) sts from rem st holder. Work 2(2;2,5) cm st st on 64(66;74) sts on N. Dec 1 st (7 sts in from each end) and 1 st each side of centre 12(14;14) sts on next and follow alt row. Work 1 row straight. C/off.

TO MAKE UP
Stitch side seams.

Bonnet

Using 3 mm Ns, c/on 88(92;96) sts and work 8 cm in K1, P1 rib. Change to 3,25 mm Ns and cont in st st. C/off 3 sts at beg of next 2 rows. Cont straight until work measures 20(21;22) cm from beg. C/off 23(24;25) sts at beg of next 2 rows. Cont on centre 36(38;40) sts for a further 9(9,5;10) cm. C/off.

TO MAKE UP
Stitch seams at top of bonnet. Using 3 mm Ns, pick up and K90(94;98) sts around front edge and work 3 rows K1, P1 rib. C/off. Stitch the row ends of these 3 rows to 3 c/off sts of lower rib on right side. Fold rib in half, lengthwise, to right side.

Layette with stripes

MATERIALS

Confort (50 g balls); **Jumpsuit:** 6(6;7) balls Ecru (A), 1 ball each Red (B), Yellow (C) and Green (D); **Mitts and Hat:** 1 ball A for each; oddments B, C and D; **Sweater:** 3(3;4) balls A; oddments B, C and D. One pair each 2,75 mm and 3,5 mm knitting needles; 8 buttons for jumpsuit; 4 buttons for sweater.

MEASUREMENTS

Jumpsuit and Sweater: to fit baby of 9(12;18) months; **Mitts and Hat:** 9-12(18) months; **Jumpsuit:** length to back neck 61(66;71) cm; sleeve length 21(23;25) cm; **Sweater:** actual all round measurement 51(56;61) cm; length to back neck 28(31;34) cm; sleeve length 22(24;27) cm.

TENSION

24 sts and 32 rows = 10 cm over patt using 3,5 mm Ns.

PATT ST

Irish Moss Stitch (IM), worked on an odd number of sts as follows:
First row (right side): K1, * P1, K1; rep from * to end.
2nd and 3rd rows: P1, * K1, P1; rep from * to end.
4th row (wrong side): As first.
These 4 rows form one patt.

Jumpsuit

MAIN PART

Beg at lower edge of left leg c/on 47(51;55) sts using 2,75 mm Ns and B. Work in rib as fols:
First row (right side): P1, * K1, P1; rep from * to end.
2nd row: K1, * P1, K1; rep from * to end. Cont in rib working 2 more rows in B, then 4 rows C, 4 rows D, 4 rows B, 4 rows C and 4 rows D. Change to 3,5 mm Ns and A.
Inc row: P1 [inc in next st] 44(48;52) times, P2. [91;99;107) sts.] This row reverses ribbed border to allow for turn-up. Now work in IM as given above and cont without shaping until work measures 12(13;14) cm from beg. Inc 1 st at both ends of next row, then every fol 8th row 2(3;4) times, then at both ends of every fol 6th row 3(2;1) times working extra sts into patt. Cont on 103(111;119) sts until work measures 25(27;29) cm from beg, ending with a 4th patt row.

CROTCH SHAPING

C/off 3 sts at beg of next 2 rows, 2 sts at beg of next 2 rows and 1 st at beg of next 6 rows. There are 87(95;103) sts, ending with a 2nd patt row. ★★ Cut yarn and leave sts on a spare N. Work right leg in same way as far as ★★.
3rd row of patt: [P1, K1] 43(47;51) times, then P rem st of right leg tog with first st of left leg, [K1, P1] 43(47;51) times. [173 (189;205) sts.] Patt rows now fit correctly beg with 4th row. Cont in patt across all sts until work measures 50(54;58) cm from beg, ending with a RS row. Divide for armholes as fols:
Next row: P8(9;10), [P2tog, P8(9;10)] 3 times and leave these 35(39;43) sts of left front on a holder, c/off 10, P until there are 5 sts on right N after armhole, [P2tog, P7(8;9)] 8 times and leave these 69(77;85) sts of back on another holder, c/off 10, P until there are 8(9;10) sts on right N after armhole, [P2tog, P8(9;10)] 3 times. Cont on 35(39;43) sts now rem on N for right front. ★★★ Change to 2,75 mm Ns and work in rib as on leg border but using A only; cont until work measures 58(62;67) cm from beg, ending at front edge.

NECK SHAPING

C/off 6(7;8) sts at beg of next row, 4 sts at same edge on next alt row, 2 sts on next 2(2;3) alt rows and 1 st on next 2(3;2) alt rows. Cont on rem 19(21;23) sts until work measures 62(67;72) cm from beg. C/off loosely RW. ★★★

BACK

With RS facing and using 2,75 mm Ns and A rejoin to 69(77;85) sts of back and work in rib as on leg border but using A only. Cont until work measures 61(66;71) cm from beg, ending with a WS row.

NECK SHAPING

First row: Rib 22(24;26) and leave these sts of right back, c/off next 25(29;33) sts RW; rib to end. Cont on 22(24;26) sts now rem at end of N for left back and work 1 row straight. C/off 3 sts at beg of next row then c/off rem 19(21;23) sts loosely RW for shoulder edge. Rejoin yarn to neck edge of right back sts, c/off 3, rib to end. Work 1 row on rem 19(21;23) sts then c/off loosely RW.

LEFT FRONT

With RS facing and using 2,75 mm Ns and A rejoin to 35(39;43) sts of left front and complete as for right front from ★★★ to ★★★ rev shapings.

SLEEVES

With 2,75 mm Ns and B c/on 35(37;41) sts. Work in rib as on leg border but beg with 2nd rib row; work 4 rows in B, 4 rows in C and 4 rows in D thus ending with a first rib row. Change to 3,5 mm Ns and A.
Inc row: P 5(1;5), [inc in next st, P2] 10(12;12) times. [45(49;53) sts.] Now work in IM patt but inc 1 st at both ends of every fol 8th row 1(4;7) times, then every fol 6th row 6(3;0) times working extra sts into patt. Cont on 59(63;67) sts until work measures 21(23;25) cm from beg. C/off all sts.

MAKE UP AND BORDERS

Join shoulder seams. With RS of work facing and using 2,75 mm Ns and D, pick up and K17(21;23) sts round right front neck edge, 35(39;43) sts across back neck and 17(21;23) sts down left front neck. Beg with 2nd row work in rib working 1 row in D, 2 rows in C and 1 row in B. C/off loosely RW using B.

Join centre front seam along the shaped crotch edges. With RS of work facing and using 2,75 mm Ns and D, pick up and K83(89;97) sts along remainder of right front edge including edge of neck border. Rep 2nd rib row then change to C and make buttonholes.
Next row: Beg at lower edge rib 9(8;9), c/off 1, [rib until there are 9(10;11) sts on right N after previous buttonhole, c/off 1] 7 times, rib to end. On fol row c/on 1 st over each buttonhole. Change to B and rib to end, then c/off loosely RW using B. On left front edge pick up same numbers of sts using D and rib 1 row then c/off loosely RW. Join sleeve seams leaving 7 rows open at top. Sew cast-off edge of sleeves to sides of armholes and join the open section at top to armhole cast-off placing sleeve seam in centre of this cast-off space. Join crotch seam on back. Join inner leg seams reversing seam on lower half of border for turn-up. Lap right front border over edge of left front and sew lower edge in place. Sew on buttons to correspond with buttonholes.

Hat

With 3,5 mm Ns and B c/on 91(101) sts. Work in rib beg with first row and work [4 rows B, 4 rows C, 4 rows D] twice. Change to A and P 1 row thus reversing brim. Now work in IM patt and cont without shaping until work measures 15(17) cm from beg, ending with a 4th patt row. Shape top as fols:

First row: Patt 4, [SKTPO, patt 5] 10(11) times, SKTPO, patt 4(6). Rep 2nd patt row.

3rd row: [patt 3, SKTPO] 11(12) times, patt 3(5). Rep 4th patt row.

5th row: K1, P1, [SKTPO, P1] 11(12) times, patt 1(3). Rep 2nd patt row.

7th row: [P2tog, K2tog] 6(7) times, P1. Cut yarn, thread end through rem 13 sts, draw up tightly and sew securely then join seam reversing it on brim.

Crew-neck sweater

BACK

With 2,75 mm Ns and B c/on 61(67;73) sts and work in rib.

First row (right side): P1, * K1, P1; rep from * to end.

2nd row: K1, * P1, K1; rep from * to end. Cont in rib working 1 more row in B then 4 rows in C and 4 rows in D. Change to 3,5 mm Ns and A; P 1 row on wrong side then work in IM patt as given above. Cont without shaping until work measures 17(19;21) cm from beg, ending with a WS row.

ARMHOLE SHAPING

C/off 5 sts at beg of next 2 rows **. Cont on rem 51(57;63) sts until work measures 28(31;34) cm from beg, ending with a RS row.

NECK SHAPING

Next row: Patt 13(15;17) and leave these sts of left back on a holder, c/off next 25(27;29) sts, patt to end. Cont on 13(15;17) sts now rem on N for right back. Change to 2,75 mm Ns and work in rib as on welt beg with first row; work 1 row in D, 2 rows in C and 1 row in B. C/off loosely RW using B. With RS facing and using 2,75 mm Ns and D, rejoin to sts of left back and work similar border.

FRONT

Work as for back to ** and cont until 12 rows fewer have been worked in patt thus ending with a WS row.

NECK SHAPING

First row: Patt 21 (23;25) and leave these sts of left front on a spare N, c/off next 9(11;13) sts, patt to end. Cont on 21(23;25) sts now rem on N for right front and work 1 row straight. *** C/off 3 sts at beg of next row, 2 sts at same edge on next alt row and 1 st on next 3 alt rows. *** Work 1 row on rem 13(15;17) sts then change to 2,75 mm Ns and D. Rep first rib row then change to C.

2nd row: Rib 7(8;9), c/off 1, rib to end. On fol row c/on 1 st over buttonhole. Rib 1 row in B then c/off loosely RW in B.

With WS facing rejoin A to sts of left front. Cont as for right front from *** to *** then work 2 rows straight. Change to 2,75 mm Ns and D. Rep first rib row then change to C.

2nd row: Rib 5(6;7), c/off 1, rib to end. Complete as for right front border.

SLEEVES

With 2,75 mm Ns and B c/on 35(39;41) sts and work the 11 rows of striped rib as on welt. Change to 3,5 mm Ns and A.

Inc row (wrong side): [P11(7;5), inc in next st] 2(4;6) times, P11(7;5). [37(43; 47) sts.] Now work in IM patt but inc 1 st at both ends of every fol 6th (6th;8th) row 5(7;3) times, then every fol 4th (4th;6th) row 4(2;6) times. Cont on 55(61;65) sts until work measures 22 (24;27) cm from beg. C/off all sts.

NECK BORDERS

With RS of work facing and using 2,75 mm Ns and D, pick up and K33(35;37) sts round back neck edge including ends of shoulder borders. Beg with 2nd row work in rib working 1 row in D, 2 rows in C and 1 row in B. C/off loosely RW using B.

With RS facing and using 2,75 mm Ns and D, pick up and K43(45;47) sts round front neck edge including ends of shoulder borders. Rep 2nd rib row then change to C.

Next row: Rib 3, c/off 1, rib to last 4 sts, c/off 1, rib to end. On fol row c/on 1 st over each buttonhole. Change to B and rib 1 row then c/off loosely RW using B.

TO MAKE UP

Lap front shoulder borders over back borders and oversew at sides. Sew cast-off edge of sleeves to sides of armholes and armhole cast-off to a corresponding depth on sides of sleeves. Join side and sleeve seams. Sew on buttons to correspond with buttonholes.

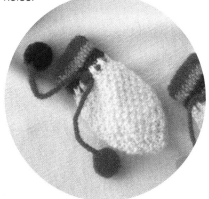

Mittens

Make 2 alike. With 2,75 mm Ns and B c/on 39(43) sts and work in rib as given above beg with first row. Work 2 rows in B, then 3 rows in C and 3 rows in D. Change to 3,5 mm Ns and A. K 1 row.

Next row: P2, [yrn, P2tog] 18(20) times, P1. Now work in IM patt as given above and work 20(24) rows thus ending with a 4th patt row. Shape top as fols:

First row: Patt 5(3), [P3tog, patt 5] 4(5) times, patt 2(0). Work 3 rows on rem 31(33) sts.

5th row: Patt 4(2), [SKTPO, patt 3] 4(5) times, patt 3(1). Work 3 rows on rem 23 sts.

9th row: Patt 3(1), [P3tog, K1] 5 times, patt 0(2). Cut yarn, thread end through rem 13 sts, draw up tightly and sew securely, then join side seam. Make a twisted cord about 30 cm long using B and thread it through holes at wrist. Make 2 small pompons, one in C and 1 in D and attach one to each end.

Baby in grey

MATERIALS
Confort (50 g balls); **Sweater:** 2(3;3) balls Grey (A); 1 ball Pink (B) and Green (C); **Trousers:** 3(3;4;4) balls A; oddments of B and C; **Hat:** 2(2;3) balls A; oddments of B and C; one pair each 2,75 mm, 3 mm and 3,75 mm knitting needles; one set each 3 mm and 3,75 mm double-pointed knitting needles; 6 buttons for sweater; 2 buttons and shirring elastic for trousers; 1 button for hat.

MEASUREMENTS
To fit baby 3-6(9-12;15-18) months; actual all round measurement: **Sweater** 48(54;57) cm; length to back neck 24(27;30) cm; sleeve seam 16(18;20) cm; **Trousers** length 28(31;33;36) cm.

TENSION
Sweater and Mitts: 23 sts and 30 rows = 10 cm using st st and 3,75 mm Ns.
Trousers and Hat: 23 sts and 42 rows = 10 cm using Fisherman's Rib and 3 mm Ns.

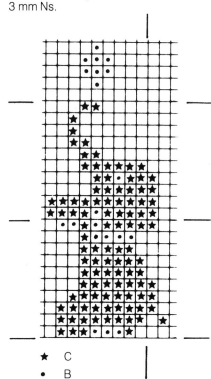

★ C
• B

Sweater

BACK
Using 2,75 mm Ns and B, c/on 55(61; 65) sts and work in K1, P1 rib as fols: 2 rows in B, 6 rows in A and 2 rows in C. Change to 3,75 mm Ns and A. Beg with K row work in st st, inc 1 st at centre of first row. [56(62;66) sts.] Cont straight until work measures 14(16;18) cm from beg, ending with a P row.

SHAPE RAGLAN
C/off 2 sts at beg of next 2 rows. Work 1 row straight then dec 1 st at each end of next 3 rows. Rep last 4 rows 3 times more. [28(34;38) sts.] Dec 1 st at each end of next 6(8;9) alt rows. C/off rem 16(18;20) sts.

FRONT
Work as for back until 26(28;30) sts rem, ending with a P row.

SHAPE NECK
Keeping raglan shaping correct, patt until there are 8 sts on right N. Join 2nd ball of yarn, c/off 8(10;12) sts, K to end. Dec 1 st at each neck edge on next 3 rows then on fol alt row. C/off rem 2 sts. Note: front is 4 rows shorter than back.

LEFT SLEEVE
Using 2,75 mm Ns and B, c/on 31(33;35) sts and work the 10 rows of striped rib as on back, then change to 3,75 mm Ns and A.
Inc row: K3(1;2), [inc in next st, K5(4;4)] 4(6;6) times, inc in next st, K3(1;2). [36(40;42) sts.] Cont in st st, inc 1 st at each end of every fol 6th row 0(2;3) times, every fol 4th row (7 times), then every fol 3rd row 2(0;0) times. [54(58; 62) sts.] Cont straight until work measures 16(18;20) cm from beg, ending with a P row.

SHAPE RAGLAN
Work as for back raglan from ** to ** then dec 1 st at each end of next 4(6;7) alt rows. [18(18;20) sts.]

SHAPE SLEEVE TOP
Work 1 row straight then on fol row c/off 6 sts at beg and dec 1 st at end. Rep last 2 rows once. C/off rem 4(4;6) sts.

RIGHT SLEEVE
Work as for left sleeve rev top shaping on last 4 rows.

MAKE UP AND BORDERS
Stitch back raglan seams. With RS facing, using 2,75 mm Ns and A, pick up and K13(13;15) sts across top edge of right sleeve, 15(17;19) sts across back neck and 13(13;15) sts across top of left sleeve. Work 3 rows K1, P1 rib. C/off loosely RW. With RS facing, using 2,75 mm Ns and A, pick up and K25(27;29) sts around front neck edge, work as for back neck border. Stitch front raglan seams for a depth of 4 cm from lower edge. Stitch side and sleeve seams. With RS facing, using 2,75 mm Ns and A, pick up and K23(25;27) sts along remainder of left front raglan edge including edge of border, rib 1 row.
Next row (buttonholes): Rib 4, * c/off 2 [rib until there are 5(6;7) sts on right N after previous buttonhole, c/off 2] twice, rib to end. On fol row c/on 2 sts over each buttonhole. Rib 1 more row then c/off RW. Pick up same number of sts on right front raglan edge and rib 1 row.
Next row: Beg at neck edge rib 3, then rep from * in same row of previous border to end. Complete buttonholes on next row, rib 1 row then c/off RW. On edges of sleeves pick up same numbers of sts, rib 1 row then c/off RW. Now embroider motif: on front mark centre of work, 4 rows before start of raglan and beg on next row embroider motif in cross st working from graph. Lap front armhole borders over edges of sleeves and catch in place at base of openings. Sew on buttons.

Trousers

BACK
For one leg c/on 31(33;35;37) sts using 2,75 mm Ns and B. Work in K1, P1 rib, as fols:
1 row in B, 25 rows in A, 2 rows in C. Change to A.
Inc row: Rib 3(5;5;7), [d inc, rib 5] 4 times, d inc, rib 3(3;5;5). [41(43;45;47) sts.] Change to 3 mm Ns and patt as fols:
First row (right side): K.
2nd row: K1, * P1, K1 below; rep from * to last 2 sts, P1, K1. These 2 rows form patt. Cont until work measures 10(11; 11;12) cm from beg, ending with a first patt row **. Cut yarn and leave sts on a spare N. Work second leg in same way to **, then join the legs as fols;
Patt 40(42;44;46) sts of second leg then K rem st tog with first st of first leg, patt 40(42;44;46). [81(85;89;93) sts.]

SHAPE CROTCH
First row: K37(39;41;43), K3tog, K1, SKTPO, K37(39;41;43).
2nd row: As 2nd patt row.
3rd row: K35(37;39;41), K3tog, K1, SKTPO, K35(37;39;41). Cont in patt on rem 73(77;81;85) sts until work measures 25(28;30;33) cm from beg, ending with a first patt row.
Dec row: Rib 9(11;13;15), [P3tog, patt 15] 3 times, P3tog, patt 7(9;11;13).

[65(69;73;77) sts.] Change to 2,75 mm Ns and work 4 rows K1, P1 rib.

5th row (buttonholes): Rib 18(20;20; 22), c/off 2, rib to last 20(22;22;24) sts, c/off 2, rib to end. On fol row, c/on 2 sts over each buttonhole. Work 4 more rows then c/off loosely RW.

FRONT
Work as for back omitting buttonholes in waistband.

SHOULDER STRAPS (make 2)
Using 2,75 mm Ns and A, c/on 7 sts.
First row: K2 [P1, K1] twice, K1.
2nd row: [K1, P1] 3 times, K1.
Rep these 2 rows until work measures 40 cm from beg. C/off RW.

TO MAKE UP
Stitch inner leg and side seams rev seams on leg borders. Fold borders to RS. Stitch shoulder straps to front waistband allowing band to overlap strap for 4 rows. Sew a button to other end of each strap. Thread shirring elastic thread through waistband, securing ends at a side seam.

Hat

MAIN PART
Beg with neck border, using 2,75 mm Ns and A, c/on 83(87;91) sts, work 7 rows K1, P1 rib.
Next row (buttonholes): Rib to last 5 sts, c/off 2, rib to end. On fol row c/on 2 sts over buttonhole. Work 16 rows in

rib, then make another buttonhole on next 2 rows. Work 7 more rows in rib.
Next row: C/off 12 sts loosely RW, rib until there are 59(63;67) sts on right N, then c/off rem 12 sts loosely RW and fasten off. With RS of work facing and using 3 mm Ns, rejoin A to rem 59(63; 67) sts and work in patt as given for trousers until work measures 22(23; 24) cm from beg. C/off 20(22;22) sts at beg of next 2 rows. Cont on rem 19(19; 23) sts for upper section until sides of this section measure 8,5(9,5;9,5) cm. C/off.

MAKE UP AND FRONT BORDER
Stitch sides of the upper section to the groups of 20(22;22) cast-off sts at each side. With RS facing, using 2,75 mm Ns and A, pick up and K83(87;95) sts all around front edge of hat leaving lower border free. Work in K1, P1 rib as fols:
1 row in A, 2 rows in C, 7 rows in A, 4 rows in B, 7 rows in A and 1 row in C. C/off RW. Fold this border to RS folding along centre of the 4 rows worked in B and tack in place. Fold the lower border in half to RS and neatly oversew along front edges and the groups of 12 cast-off sts at each side through double thickness. Catch side edge of the front border to cast-on edge of neck border then leave remainder of both borders free. Buttonhole-stitch around the double buttonhole. Sew on button.

Mittens

LEFT MITT
Using set of 3 mm dp Ns and B, c/on 28(30;32) sts and work in rounds of K1, P1 rib, 1 round in B, 4 rounds in A and 2 rounds in C. Change to set of 3,75 mm dp Ns and using A work in rounds of st st. After working 2 rounds shape for thumb.
3rd row: K12(13;14) then pick up lp lying between Ns and K it through the back – referred to as K lp, K2, K lp, K14(15;16).
4th round: K without shaping.
5th round: K12(13;14), K lp, K4, K lp, K14(15;16). Cont to inc in these positions on next 2 alt rounds working 2 extra sts between incs each time, then

work 1 round on 36(38;40) sts.
11th round: K12(13;14) and place these sts on a piece of contrast yarn, K next 10 sts, turn and place rem 14(15; 16) sts on another piece of contrast yarn. C/on 2 sts, turn. Join the 12 sts into a ring and cont for thumb, working 6(8;9) rounds in st st then shape top.
Next round: [K1, K2tog] 4 times. K 1 round.
Next round: [K2tog] 4 times. Cut yarn and pass end through rem sts, draw up tightly and sew securely then darn in end. With RS facing pick up and K2 sts on the cast-on edge at base of thumb, then K the rem 14(15;16) sts left unworked at end of 11th round. Cont in rounds on these 28(30;32) sts until work measures 8(9;10) cm from beg.

SHAPE TOP
First round: * K1, SKPO, K8(9;10), K2tog, K1; rep from * once.
2nd round: K without shaping.
3rd round: * K1, SKPO, K6(7;8) K2tog, K1; rep from * once. Cont to dec in these positions on next 3 alt rounds working 2 sts less between pairs of decs each time. Cut yarn, thread end through rem 8(10;12) sts, draw up tightly and sew securely.

RIGHT MITT
Work as for left mitt, rev position of thumb by reading the thumb rows in rev. On back of each mitt mark the centre and work the small motifs from chart, working in cross-st.

V-Neck sweater

MATERIALS
Corrida 3 (50 g balls); 3(4;4;5;6) balls; one pair each 2,25 mm and 3 mm knitting needles.

MEASUREMENTS
To fit chest 56(61;66;71;76) cm; actual all round measurement 62(65;69;76; 80) cm; length to shoulder 28(29;33; 37;41) cm; sleeve length 25(27;30;33; 36) cm.

TENSION
28 sts and 42 rows = 10 cm using patt st and 3 mm Ns.

STITCHES USED
Zig-zag patt: worked on a multiple of 5 sts plus 2 as fols:
First row (right side): K2, * P3, K2 *; rep from * to *.
2nd row: P1 * K3, P2 *; rep from * to * ending K1.
3rd row: P2, * K2, P3 *; rep from * to *.
4th row: K2, * P2, K3 *; rep from * to *.
5th row: K1, * P3, K2 *; rep from * to * ending P1.
6th row: P.
7th row: K.
8th row: K1, * P2, K3 *; rep from * to * ending P1.
9th row: * P3, K2 *; rep from * to * ending P2.
10th row: * K3, P2 *; rep from * to * ending K2.
11th row: P1, * K2, P3 *; rep from * to * ending K1.
12th row: P2, * K3, P2 *; rep from * to *.
These 12 rows form one patt.

BACK
Using 2,25 mm Ns, c/on 87(91;97; 107;111) sts and work 4 cm K1, P1 rib, inc 0(1;0;0;1) st in centre of last row. [87(92;97;107;112) sts.]
Change to 3 mm Ns and cont in patt until work measures 16(16;19;22;25) cm from beg, ending with a WS row. V**.

SHAPE ARMHOLES
C/off 5(5;5;7;7) sts at beg of next 2 rows. [77(82;87;93;98) sts.] Cont straight until work measures 28(29;33;37;41) cm from beg, ending with a WS row.

SHAPE SHOULDERS AND NECK
C/off 6(7;8;9;10) sts at beg of next 2 rows.
Next row: C/off 6(7;8;9;10) sts, patt until there are 10 sts on right N, leave these sts for right back, c/off next 33(34;35; 37;38) sts, patt to end. Cont on

16(17;18;19;20) sts now rem at end of N for left back. C/off 6(7;8;9;10) sts at beg of next row and 2 sts at neck edge of fol row. C/off rem 8 sts. Rejoin yarn to neck edge of right back sts, c/off 2 sts, patt to end. C/off rem 8 sts.

FRONT
Work as for back to **.

SHAPE ARMHOLES AND NECK
Next row: C/off 5(5;5;7;7) sts, patt until there are 38(41;43;46;49) sts on right N, leave these sts of left front on a spare N, c/off 1(0;1;1;0), patt to end. Cont on 43(46;48;53;56) sts rem on N for right front and c/off 5(5;5;7;7) sts at beg of next row.*** Dec 1 st at neck edge on next and fol 7(6;2;1;0) alt rows, then on every fol 3rd row 10(12;16;18;20) times. Cont straight until work matches back to beg of shoulder, ending at side.

SHAPE SHOULDERS
C/off 6(7;8;9;10) sts at beg of next and fol alt row, work 1 row then c/off rem 8 sts. Rejoin yarn to neck edge of left front sts, patt to end. Complete as for right front from *** to end.

SLEEVES
Using 2,25 mm Ns, c/on 41(43;47; 47;51) sts and work 4 cm K1, P1 rib inc 11(14;15;15;16) sts evenly across last row. [52(57;62;62;67) sts.] Change to 3 mm Ns and cont in patt, inc 1 st at each end of every fol 12th row 7(0;6;0;0) times, then every fol 10th row 0(8;2;7;11) times, then every fol 8th row 0(0;0;4;0) times, working extra sts into patt. [66(73;78;84;89) sts.] Cont straight until work measures 25(27;30; 33;36) cm from beg. V. C/off loosely.

MAKE UP AND NECKBAND
Stitch right shoulder seam. With RS facing and using 2,25 mm Ns, pick up and K48(50;53;57;60) sts down left front neck edge, 1 st from centre 'V', 48(50;53;57;60) sts up right front neck and 37(38;39;41;42) sts across back neck. [134(139;146;156;163) sts.] Work 1 row K1, P1 rib, keeping rib correct, dec 1 st at each side of centre 'V' on next 5 rows. C/off loosely RW. Stitch cast off edge of sleeves to sides of armholes and sew armhole cast off to a corresponding depth on sides of sleeves. Stitch side and sleeve seams matching patt. DO NOT IRON.

Fancy knits

Sweater with dotted yoke

MATERIALS
Classic Super 4; 5(5;6) balls Ecru (A), oddments of Yellow (B), Green (C), Red (D), Grey (E). One pair each 2,75 mm and 3 mm knitting needles; 1 cable needle.

MEASUREMENTS
To fit chest 56(61;66) cm.

STITCHES USED
Double moss stitch:
First row: *K 1, P 1 *.
2nd and every even row: Work sts as set, i.e. K the P sts and P the K sts of previous row.
3rd row: * P 1, K 1 *.
5th row: Repeat from first row.

Cable over 4 sts:
First row: K 4.
2nd row: P 4.
3rd row: Slip 2 sts onto cable needle and leave at front of work, K the next 2 sts, then K the 2 sts from cable needle. Repeat this cable twist every 4 rows.
Coloured dots: Using a short length of separate colour yarn, work 7 sts into 1 st as fols: K1, P1, K1, P1, K1, P1, K1 then c/off the 6th st over the 7th st, the 5th st over the 6th st, etc. until 1 st rems.

TENSION
30 sts and 42 rows = 10 cm using double moss stitch and 3 mm Ns.

BACK
Using 2,75 mm Ns and A, c/on 92(98;104) sts and work as fols: 2 sts in rev st st, * 1 cable, 2 sts in rev st st *; rep from * to * 15(16;17) times in all. When work measures 5 cm change to 3 mm Ns and cont in double moss st, inc 1 st on the first row. [93(99;105) sts.] When work measures 21(23; 25) cm **shape armholes:** c/off 3 sts at the beg of next 2 rows, then 2 sts at the beg of next 4 rows, then 1 st at the beg of next 6(8;10) rows.

Now work 1 row of dots as fols: work 3(5;7) sts in double moss st, work 1 dot in B, * 10 sts in double moss st, 1 dot in C, 10 sts in double moss st, 1 dot in B *: rep from * to * 3 times in all, then end with 3(5;7) sts in double moss st. Work 1 row with 1 inc above each dot. On the next row above each dot start: 1 cable which is crossed on the third row: 7 cables with 8 sts between. On the 2nd row following the 3rd cable twist row, work 1 row of dots as fols: 2(4;6) sts in double moss st, * 1 cable, 4 sts in

double moss st, 1 dot in D, 3 sts in double moss st, 1 cable, 4 sts in double moss st, 1 dot in E, 3 sts in double moss st *: rep from * to * 3 times in all. End with 1 cable and 2(4;6) sts in double moss st. Work 1 row: on the next row, work rev st st between the cables and **at the same time**, above each dot, work 2 incs and form 1 cable which will be crossed on the 3rd row. [92(96;100) sts.] (13 cables with 3 sts between them).

When work measures 34(37;40) cm **shape shoulders**: (reduce the cables by 2 sts at the same time, = 8 extra decs each side): c/off 7(8;8) sts at the beg of next 2 rows.

Next row: c/off 7(7;8) sts at the beg of row, then c/off centre 12(14;16) sts for neck on the same row (reducing the cables by 2 sts = 10 extra decs), work to end of row. Cont on this side only. C/off 7(7;8) sts at the beg of next row. C/off 6 sts at the beg of next row (neck shaping). C/off 7 sts at the beg of next row. Complete other side to match, rev all shapings.

FRONT
Work as given for back.
When work measures 29(32;35) cm **shape neck** (reducing the cables by 2 sts = 10 extra decs): c/off centre 6 sts, then cont each side separately. C/off at neck edge on every alt row as fols: 3 sts 1(1;2) times, 2 sts 2(2;1) times and 1 st 2(3;3) times. When work measures 34(37;40) cm work the 3 shoulder shapings as given for one side of back. Complete other side to match, rev all shapings.

SLEEVES
Using 2,75 mm Ns and A, c/on 50(56;62) sts and work as fols: 2 sts in rev st st, * 1 cable, 2 sts in rev st st * rep from * to * 8(9;10) times in all. Cont thus for 5 cm working 1 inc in centre of last row. Change to 3 mm Ns and cont in double moss st, inc 1 st at each end of every fol 7th(8th;9th) row 10 times. [71(77;83) sts.]

When work measures 24(26;28) cm **shape armholes**: c/off 3 sts at the beg of next 2 rows, and 2 sts at the beg of next 4 rows. Now work a row of dots as fols: C/off 2, work in double moss st until there are 4(7;10) sts on right N, * 1 dot in C, 10 sts in double moss st, 1 dot in B, 10 sts in double moss st *, rep from * to * again, 1 dot in C and rem 6(9;12) sts in double moss st. On fol row c/off 2 sts at beg and work 1 inc over each dot. [58(64;70) sts.]

3rd row: Work 3(6;9) sts in double moss st, * K4 to form a cable which will be crossed on next alt row, work 8 sts in double moss st * rep from * to * 4 times in all, K4 to form a cable, work 3(6;9) sts in double moss st. Cont as now set but dec 1 st at both ends of next row and next 7(9;11) WS rows. Meanwhile on 15th row of patt work another line of dots between the cables in same way as on back and front then on 17th row replace the double moss st by rev st st and also work 2 incs over each dot and form a cable in same way as on back and front; you thus form 4 new cables adding 8 extra sts. After decs have been completed c/off 2 sts at beg of next 6 rows, then 3 sts at beg of next 6 rows. C/off rem 20(22;24) sts.

TO MAKE UP
Stitch right shoulder seam.

NECK BORDER
Using 2,75 mm Ns and A, pick up and K approximately 50(52;54) sts around front neck, then 28(30;32) sts across back neck. Work 6 rows in single rib. C/off.

LEFT SHOULDER BORDERS (2)
Using 2,75 mm Ns and A, pick up and K24(25;26) sts across the left front shoulder and work in single rib. On the 2nd row, work 2 buttonholes (2 sts wide): the first is worked 10 sts in from armhole edge, the 2nd spaced 7(8;9) sts from the first. C/off on the 5th row.
Work a 2nd border on the back edge, omitting buttonholes.
Stitch side seams.
Lap the front left shoulder border over the back.
Stitch sleeve seams. Sew in sleeves. Sew on buttons.

Sweater with Fair Isle yoke

MATERIALS
France +; 4(5;6) balls Ecru (A); 1 ball each Khaki (B), Maroon (C) and Blue (D). One pair each 2,75 mm, 3,25 mm and 3,75 mm knitting needles.

MEASUREMENTS
To fit chest 56(61;66) cm.

STITCHES USED
Fair Isle stocking stitch: Work from the chart.
Pattern stitch: Work from the chart.

TENSION
26 sts and 36 rows = 10 cm using pattern stitch and 3,25 mm Ns.

BACK
Using 2,75 mm Ns, c/on 79(83;87) sts and work 4 cm in single rib. Change to 3,25 mm Ns and cont in patt st, beg as shown on the chart, and inc 0(4;8) sts evenly across first row. [79(87;95) sts.] When work measures 22(25;27) cm **shape armholes**: c/off 2 sts at the beg of next 2 rows, then 1 st at the beg of next 6(10;14) rows. Leave rem 69(73;77) sts on spare N.

FRONT
Work as given for back. When work measures 22(25;27) cm work the same armhole shapings as given for back. **At the same time**, when working the 2nd (6th;10th) armhole shaping row, shape yoke: leave centre 29(33;37) sts on spare N and complete each side separately, leaving sts at centre edge of work on spare N on every alt row as fols: 8 sts (once), 7 sts (once), 5 sts (once). Leave rem 69(73;77) sts on spare N.

Yoke

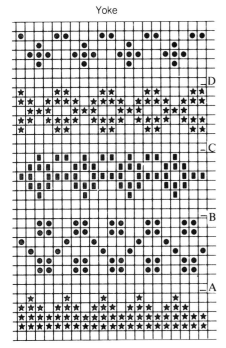

Pattern stitch

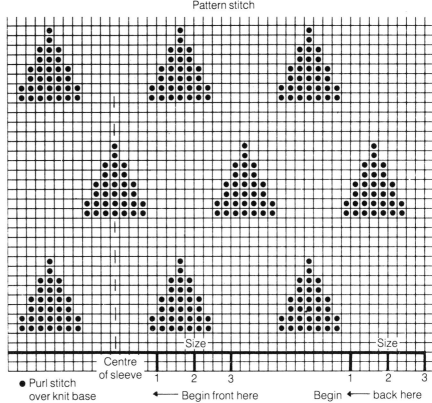

★ Blue

● Maroon

▌ Khaki

● Purl stitch over knit base

Centre of sleeve

Size

1 2 3

← Begin front here

Size

1 2 3

Begin ← back here

SLEEVES

Using 2,75 mm Ns, c/on 43(49; 55) sts and work 5 cm in single rib. Change to 3,25 mm Ns and cont in patt st, inc 14(16;18) sts evenly across first row. [57(65;73) sts.] Cont by inc 1 st at each end of every 14th row (4 times). [65(73;81) sts.] When work measures 25(27;29) cm **shape armholes:** work the same shapings as given for back. Leave rem 55(59;63) sts on spare N.

YOKE

Using 3,75 mm Ns, work across the sts left on back, then across one sleeve, then across the front, then across the other sleeve. [248(264;280) sts.] Using A, work 2 rows in st st, working the last st of one section together with the first st of next section on the first row, and dec 1 st in the centre of back and 1 st in the centre of each sleeve on the first row. [242(258;274) sts.]
Cont by working from the Fair Isle chart, with 1 border st at each end of work. Dec 32 sts evenly across row A. [210(226;242) sts.] Dec 33(39;45) sts evenly across row B. [177(187;197) sts.] Dec 30 sts evenly across row C. [147(157;167) sts.]
Dec 30 (35;40) sts evenly across row D. [117(122;127) sts.]

After completing chart, change to 2,75 mm Ns and A and work 5 rows in single rib, dec 20 sts evenly across first row. C/off. Stitch the yoke seam and neck ribbing seam, taking 1 st at each end into the seam. Stitch side and sleeve seams.

Cardigan with Fair Isle yoke

MATERIALS

France +; 4(4;5) balls Ecru (A), 1 ball each Khaki (B), Maroon (C) and Blue (D). One pair each 2,75 mm and 4 mm knitting needles; 6 buttons.

MEASUREMENTS

To fit chest 56(61;66) cm.

STITCHES USED

Pattern stitch: Work from chart A.
Fair Isle stocking stitch: Work from chart B, making sure you twist yarns on wrong side of work at each colour change.

TENSION

22 sts and 30 rows = 10 cm using pattern stitch and 4 mm Ns.

BACK

Using 2,75 mm Ns and A, c/on 66 (74;82) sts and work 4(5;5) cm in single rib. Change to 4 mm Ns and cont in patt st, working from chart A. When work measures 21(23;25) cm **shape armholes:** c/off 1 st at beg of every row (8 times). Leave rem 58(66;74) sts on spare N.

RIGHT FRONT

Using 2,75 mm Ns and A, c/on 30(34;38) sts and work 4(5;5) cm in single rib. Change to 4 mm Ns and cont in patt st working from chart A,

Chart A

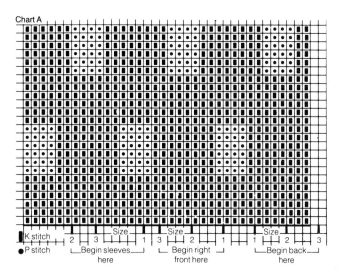

K stitch
P stitch

| 2 3 Size 1 3 Size 2 1 1 2 Size 3 |

Begin sleeves here — Begin right front here — Begin back here

Chart B

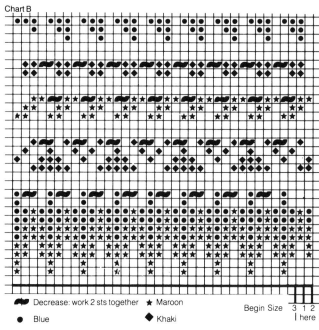

Decrease: work 2 sts together   ★ Maroon

● Blue   ◆ Khaki

Begin Size 3 1 2 here

and inc 4 sts evenly across first row. [34(38;42) sts.] When work measures 19(21;23) cm leave the fol number of sts at right hand side of work on spare N on every alt row: 8(12;16) sts (once), 6 sts (once), 3 sts (4 times), 2 sts (twice). **At the same time**, when work measures 21(23;25) cm **shape armhole:** dec 1 st at left hand side of work on every alt row (4 times). Leave rem 30(34;38) sts on spare N.

LEFT FRONT
Work as for right front, rev all shapings.

SLEEVES
Using 2,75 mm Ns and A, c/on 34(38;42) sts and work 4(5;5) cm in single rib. Change to 4 mm Ns and cont in patt st working from chart A, and inc 4(6;8) sts evenly across first row. [38(44;50) sts.] Cont by inc 1 st at each end of every 8th row (7 times). [52(58;64) sts.] When work measures 25(27;29) cm **shape armholes:** dec 1 st at each end of every alt row (4 times). Place rem 44(50;56) sts on spare N.

YOKE
Using 4 mm Ns and A, work across the sts of right front, then across one sleeve, then across the back, then across the other sleeve, then across left front. [206(234;262) sts on Ns.] Cont in Fair Isle st st, working from chart B, and inc 1 st in the centre of back on the first row, to make the Fair Isle patt symmetrical. To shape the yoke, dec as fols: on the 12th row (on the section in A between the motifs in D): dec 50(57;64) sts [157(178;199) sts.] On the 18th row (on the section in A between the motifs in B): dec 38(43;48) sts. [119(135;151) sts rem.] On the 23rd row (on the section in A between the motifs in C): dec 28(32;36) sts. [91(103;115) sts rem.] On the 27th row (on the section in A between the squares in B): dec 22(25;28) sts. [69(78;87) sts rem.] Complete work from the chart, then leave sts on spare N.

TO MAKE UP
Stitch armhole seams. Stitch side and sleeve seams.

RIGHT FRONT BORDER
Using 2,75 mm Ns and A, c/on 11 sts and work in single rib, working 5 buttonholes (3 sts wide), 3 sts in from front edge: the first is worked on 5th (7th;9th) row, the others spaced 6(6,5;7) cm apart. When work measures 31(33;35) cm leave sts on a spare N.

LEFT FRONT BORDER
Work in same way as for right front border, omitting buttonholes.
Stitch borders to fronts.

NECK BORDER
Using 2,75 mm Ns and A, work across the sts left at right front border, then work across the sts left on spare N for the yoke, dec 1 st at centre for size 2, then work across the sts left at left front border. [91(99;109) sts on Ns.] Work 2 cm in single rib, working 1 buttonhole (3 sts wide), 3 sts in from edge on the right front, 6(6,5;7) cm from the previous buttonhole. C/off. Sew on the buttons.

Fun knits

Motif sweater

MATERIALS

France + (50 g balls); 1 ball each Blue (A), Yellow (B), Red (C), Brown (D), Rust (E); 2 balls Green (F); 2(3) balls Light Blue (G). One pair 2,75 mm and one pair 3,75 mm knitting needles; 4 buttons.

MEASUREMENTS

To fit chest 61(66) cm.

STITCHES USED

Fair Isle stocking stitch: Work from the chart, making sure you twist yarns on wrong side of work at each colour change.

TENSION

25 sts and 29 rows = 10 cm using Fair Isle stocking stitch and 3,75 mm Ns.

BACK

Using 2,75 mm Ns and F, c/on 82(86) sts and work 4 cm in single rib. Change to 3,75 mm Ns and cont in Fair Isle st st, working from the corresponding chart, then cont in st st using G. **At the same time**, when work measures 23(25) cm **shape armholes**: c/off 3 sts at the beg of next 2 rows, then 2 sts at the beg of next 4 rows, then 1 st at the beg of next 4(6) rows. [64(66) sts.]
When work measures 35(38) cm, **shape shoulders and neck**: c/off 9 sts at the beg of next row, then c/off centre 20(22) sts for neck on the same row, work to end of row. Cont on this side only. C/off 9 sts at the beg of next row. C/off 5 sts at the beg of next row (neck shaping). C/off rem 8 sts at the beg of next row. Complete other side to match, rev all shapings.

FRONT

Using 2,75 mm Ns and F, c/on 82(86) sts and work 4 cm in single rib. Change to 3,75 mm Ns and cont in Fair Isle st st, working from the corresponding chart. When work measures 23(25) cm **shape armholes**: work the same shapings as given for back. [64(66) sts rem.] (When the Fair Isle chart has been completed, cont in st st using G.)

When work measures 32(36) cm **shape neck:** c/off centre 16(18) sts and cont each side separately, casting off at neck edge on every alt row as fols: 3 sts (once), 2 sts (once) and 1 st (twice). When work measures 35(38) cm **shape shoulder** for right front: with WS facing, c/off 9 sts, then 8 sts at beg of next alt row.
Complete other side to match rev all shapings.

LEFT SLEEVE

Using 2,75 mm Ns and F, c/on 40(44) sts and work 4 cm in single rib, inc 12 sts evenly across last row. [52(56) sts.] Change to 3,75 mm Ns and cont in Fair Isle st st, working from the corresponding chart, then cont in st st using G. **At the same time,** inc 1 st at each end of every 10th row (3 times), then 1 st at each end of every 12th row (3 times). [64(68) sts.] When work measures 27(29) cm **shape armholes:** c/off 3 sts at the beg of next 2 rows, then * 2 sts at the beg of next 2 rows, then 1 st at the beg of next 2 rows *: rep from * to * 5(6) times in all, then c/off 2 sts at the beg of next 2 rows, then 3 sts at the beg of next 4 rows. C/off rem 12(10) sts.

RIGHT SLEEVE

Work as given for left sleeve, but work in spots in B instead of C.

SHOULDER AND NECK BORDER

Using 2,75 mm Ns and G, pick up and K17 sts across the left front shoulder, then work 1 double st (work twice into the same st) on the corner of the shoulder and neck, 50(52) sts around front neck, work 1 double st, then 17 sts across the right shoulder. Work in single rib. On the 3rd row, work 2 buttonholes (1 st wide) on the shoulder: the first is worked 7 sts in from the armhole edge, the 2nd spaced 9 sts from the first.
C/off on the 5th row.
Work similar border on the back neck and shoulders, picking up 34(36) sts on neckline and omitting buttonholes.

TO MAKE UP

Stitch side seams.
Stitch sleeve seams. Sew in sleeves, overlapping the shoulder borders (front over back).
Sew on buttons.

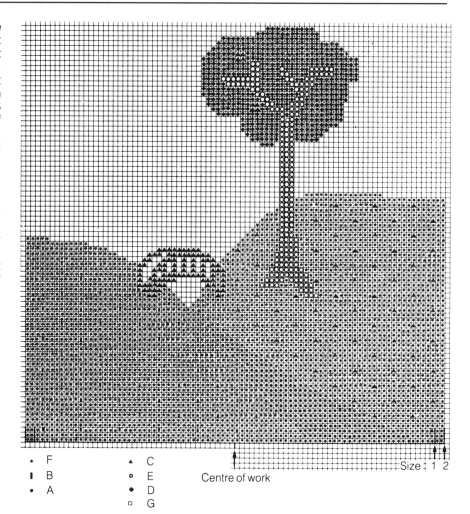

•	F	▲	C	
❙	B	○	E	
•	A	◆	D	
		▫	G	

Centre of work — Size 1 2

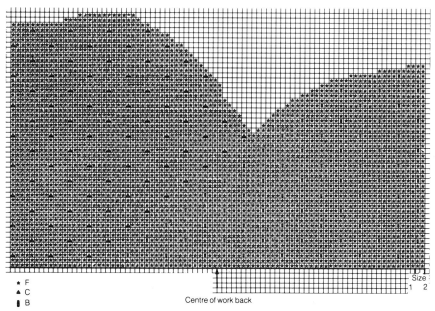

◆	F
▲	C
❙	B

Centre of work back — Size 1 2

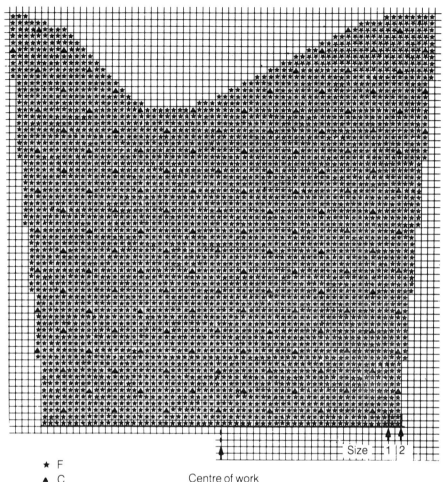

★ F
▲ C
□ G

Centre of work

When work measures 19(21;23) cm **shape armhole:** with RS facing, c/off 4(5;5) sts at the beg of the row. [34(35;37) sts rem.] When work measures 31(34;37) cm **shape shoulder:** with RS facing, c/off 6 sts at beg of next 2 alt rows, then 5 sts at beg of next alt row (c/off 6 sts at beg of next 2 alt rows, then 5 sts at beg of next alt row; c/off 6 sts at beg of next 3 alt rows). Leave rem 17(18;19) sts on spare N.

RIGHT FRONT
Work as for left front, rev all shapings.

HOOD
Using 4,5 mm Ns and A, work across the 17(18;19) sts rem on the right front, then c/on 24(26;28) sts, then work across the 17(18;19) sts rem on the left front. Work in st st, still working the 2 sts at each end in moss st. After 3 rows, work twice into each of the centre 30 sts on the next row. [88(92;96) sts.] When work measures 19(20;21) cm divide sts onto 2 Ns and graft.

TO MAKE UP
Stitch shoulder seams. Stitch hood to back neck.

Sleeveless hooded jacket

MATERIALS
Star + (50 g balls); 5(6;6) balls Red (A); 1 ball each Blue (B) and Yellow (C). One pair 3 mm and one pair 4,5 mm knitting needles; 1 open-ended zip fastener.

MEASUREMENTS
To fit chest 56(61;66) cm.

TENSION
19 sts and 24 rows = 10 cm using stocking stitch and 4,5 mm Ns.

BACK
Using 3 mm Ns and C, c/on 61(65;69) sts and work 8 cm in single rib. Change to 4,5 mm Ns and A and work in st st. When work measures 27(29;31) cm **shape armholes:** c/off 4(5;5) sts at the beg of next 2 rows. [53(55;59) sts.] When work measures 39(42;45) cm **shape shoulders:** c/off 6 sts at the beg

of next 4 rows then 5 sts at the beg of next 2 rows (c/off 6 sts at the beg of next 4 rows, then 5 sts at the beg of next 2 rows; c/off 6 sts at the beg of next 6 rows). C/off rem 19(21;23) sts.

LEFT FRONT: RIBBING AND POCKET
Using 3 mm Ns and C, c/on 30(32;34) sts and work 8 cm in single rib. Leave work on spare N.
Using 4,5 mm Ns and B, c/on 8 sts and work 6 sts at right hand side in st st, and the last 2 sts in moss st for the border. When work measures 8 cm, place the 30(32;34) sts left on spare N at right hand side of work. [38(40;42) sts on Ns.] Cont in st st using B, still working moss st border. When work measures 18 cm change to 3 mm Ns and cont in single rib. When work measures 19 cm c/off loosely RW.
Using 4,5 mm Ns and A, c/on 38(40;42) sts for the under section of the front, and work in st st, except for the last 2 sts which are worked in moss st throughout.

ARMHOLE BORDERS
Using 3 mm Ns and A, pick up and K 64(68;72) sts along side of armhole and work 8(9;9) cm in single rib. C/off.
Stitch first 6(7;7) rows of border into the base of armhole. Join rem edges of border. Fold the border in half to wrong side of work and slip stitch to back of picked up sts.
Join the front ribbing to the strip of st st. Tack the pockets to the fronts, placing the under section of the fronts level with the last row of the ribbing.

Fold the welt in two to inside of work and slip stitch in place.

Stitch zip fastener in place.

Work a fine vertical seam in the centre of each pocket on the wrong side of work to divide the pocket in two. Using C, make a pompon approximately 3 cm in diameter and attach to the zip fastener.

Number sweater

MATERIALS
Classic Confort DK (50 g balls); 4(5) balls Yellow (A); 1 ball each Red (B), Blue (C) and Green (D). One pair each 2,75 mm and 3,75 mm knitting needles; 2 buttons.

MEASUREMENTS
To fit chest 61(66) cm.

STITCHES USED
Embroidery worked in Swiss Darning.

TENSION
24 sts and 30 rows = 10 cm using stocking stitch and 3,75 mm Ns.

BACK
Using 2,75 mm Ns and A, c/on 79(87) sts and work 6 cm in single rib. Change to 3,75 mm Ns and cont in st st. When work measures 25(27) cm **shape armholes:** c/off 4 sts at the beg of next 2 rows, then 2 sts at the beg of next 2 rows, then 1 st at the beg of next 8(10) rows. [59(65) sts.]

When work measures 37(40) cm **shape shoulders and neck:** c/off 7(8) sts at beg of next row, then c/off centre 21(23) sts on the same row for neck, work to end of row. Cont on this side only. C/off 7(8) sts at beg of next row. C/off 5 sts at the beg of next row (neck shaping). C/off rem 7(8) sts at the beg

of next row. Complete other side to match, rev all shapings.

FRONT
Work as given for back.

When work measures 31(35) cm **shape neck:** c/off centre 11(13) sts and complete each side separately, casting off at neck edge on every alt row as fols: 3 sts (once), 2 sts (twice), 1 st (3 times).

When work measures 37(40) cm **shape shoulder** for right front: with WS facing c/off 7(8) sts, then 7(8) sts at beg of next alt row. Complete other side to match, rev all shapings.

SLEEVES
Using 2,75 mm Ns and A, c/on 41(45) sts and work 6 cm in single rib, inc 6(10) sts evenly across last row. [47(55) sts.] Change to 3,75 mm Ns and cont in st st, inc 1 st at each end of every 10th row (7 times). [61(69) sts.]

When work measures 30(32) cm **shape armholes:** c/off 3(4) sts at the beg of next 2 rows, then 2 sts at the beg of next 4 rows, then 1 st at the beg of next 16(20) rows, then 2 sts at the beg of

next 2 rows, then 3 sts at the beg of next 4 rows. C/off rem 15(17) sts.

TO MAKE UP
Working from the corresponding charts, embroider the numbers on the separate sections of work. Begin 18(21) cm from lower edge of back and front, and 23(26) cm from lower edge of sleeves.

Stitch right shoulder seam.

Using 2,75 mm Ns and A, pick up and K67(71) sts around neck and work 5 rows in single rib. C/off.

Using 2,75 mm Ns and A, pick up and K19(21) sts across the front left shoulder and neck border. Work 5 rows in single rib, working 2 buttonholes (2 sts wide) on the 3rd row: the first is worked 2 sts in from neck edge, the 2nd is worked 5 sts from the first. C/off on the 6th row. Work the same border omitting buttonholes across the left back shoulder but working only 2 rows. Lap front border over back edge, then sew in sleeves.

Stitch side and sleeve seams.

Sew on buttons.

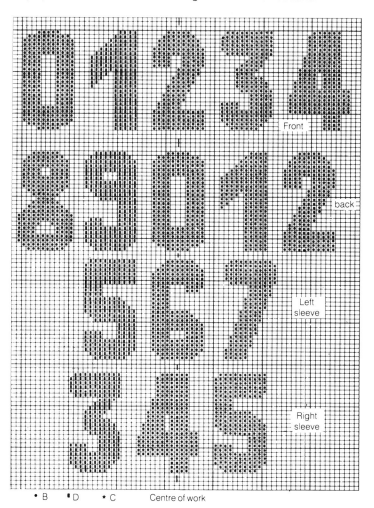

• B   ∎ D   ⋆ C   Centre of work

Child's pullover, cardigan & sweater

Child's saddle sleeve pullover

MATERIALS
Star + (50 g balls) 5(6;6) balls; one pair 3,75 mm and one pair 5 mm knitting needles.

MEASUREMENTS
To fit chest 61(66;71) cm; actual all round measurement 66(71,5;77) cm; length to back neck 34(37;40) cm; sleeve seam 27(29;31) cm.

TENSION
19 sts and 25 rows = 10 cm over st st using 5 mm Ns.

BACK
With 3,75 mm Ns c/on 58(62;66) sts and work in single rib for 5 cm working 5(6;7) incs evenly spaced along last row. [63(68;73) sts.] Change to 5 mm Ns and work in st st. Cont without shaping until work measures 23(25;27) cm from beg, ending with a P row.

ARMHOLE SHAPING
C/off 3 sts at beg of next 2 rows, 2 sts at beg of next 4 rows and 1 st at beg of next 2(4;6) rows.* Cont on rem 47(50;53) sts until work measures 34(37;40) cm from beg, ending with a P row.

SHOULDER AND NECK SHAPING
C/off 3(3;4) sts at beg of next 2 rows.
3rd row: C/off 3(3;4), K until there are 9(10;9) sts on right N, leave these for right back, c/off next 17(18;19) sts, K to end. Cont on 12(13;13) sts now rem at end of N for left back. C/off 3(3;4) sts at beg of next row and 5 sts at neck edge on fol row. C/off rem 4(5;4) sts to complete shoulder slope. Rejoin yarn to neck edge of right back sts, c/off 5, P to end. C/off rem 4(5;4) sts.

FRONT
Work as for back to * and cont until work measures 29(32;35) cm from beg, ending with a P row.

NECK AND SHOULDER SHAPING

First row: K19(20;21) and leave these sts of left front on a spare N, c/off next 9(10;11) sts, K to end. Cont on 19(20;21) sts now rem on N for right front and work 1 row straight. ** C/off 4 sts at beg of next row, 2 sts at same edge on next 2 alt rows and 1 st on next alt row. Now c/off for shoulder 3(3;4) sts at beg of next row and next alt row. Work 1 row then c/off rem 4(5;4) sts. Rejoin yarn to neck edge of left front sts. Complete as for right front from ** to end working first casting-off on next row.

Note: front is shorter than back and shapings at top of sleeves have been arranged to compensate for this.

SLEEVES

With 3,75 mm Ns c/on 32(34;36) sts and work in single rib for 5 cm working 8 incs evenly spaced along last row. [40(42;44) sts.] Change to 5 mm Ns and work in st st but inc 1 st at both ends of every fol 7th(8th;9th) row 6 times. Cont on 52(54;56) sts until work measures 27(29;31) cm from beg, ending with a P row.

TOP SHAPING

C/off 3 sts at beg of next 2 rows, 2 sts at beg of next 4 rows, 1 st at beg of next 10(12;14) rows and 2 sts at beg of next 2 rows [24 sts]. You have ended with a P row. *** C/off 2 sts at beg of next row (front edge) and 4 sts at beg of next row (back edge). C/off 4 sts at beg of next row and 6 sts at beg of fol row. Cont on rem 8 sts for shoulder yoke until side edge of this strip is the same length as right front shoulder edge. C/off. This is the right sleeve. Work left sleeve in same way as far as ***. C/off 4 sts at beg of next row (back edge) and 2 sts at beg of next row (front edge).

C/off 6 sts at beg of next row and 4 sts at beg of fol row. Cont on rem 8 sts and complete as for right sleeve.

NECKBAND

Sew shaped top edges of right sleeve to right armhole edges of front and back and sew sides of shoulder yoke section to shoulder shapings. Sew left sleeve to left front armhole and shoulder only. With RS of work facing and using 3,75 mm Ns, pick up and K80(84;88) sts all round neck edge including ends of shoulder yokes. Work in single rib for 4 rows. C/off RW.

TO MAKE UP

Join rem edges of left sleeve to back armhole and shoulder and join ends of neckband. Join side and sleeve seams.

Child's raglan sweater

MATERIALS

Confortable Fin (50 g balls) 4(4;5) balls; 2 pairs 2,75 mm and one pair 3 mm knitting needles.

MEASUREMENTS

To fit chest 51(56;61) cm; actual all round measurement 58(63,5;69) cm; length to back neck 34(38;43) cm; sleeve seam 24(26;29) cm.

TENSION

28 sts and 48 rows = 10 cm over Fisherman's Rib using 3 mm Ns.

STITCHES USED

Patt st:
First row (right side): K to end.
2nd row: K1, * P1, K1 below; rep from * to last 2 sts, P1, K1. These 2 rows form the patt.

BACK

With 2,75 mm Ns c/on 81(89;97) sts and work in single rib beg and ending RS rows with P1 and WS rows with K1. Cont until work measures 5 cm ending with a WS row. Change to 3 mm Ns and work in patt as given above. Cont until work measures 21(24;28) cm from beg, ending with a 2nd patt row.**

RAGLAN SHAPING

Place marker loops at each end of row to indicate beg of armhole. Work 4 rows straight.
5th row: K3, K3tog, K to last 6 sts, SKTPO, K3.
6th row: As 2nd patt row. Rep last 6 rows 4(4;5) times more. Now work 2 rows straight then rep 5th and 6th rows. Rep last 4 rows 7(8;8) times more. C/off rem 29(33;37) sts for back neck.

FRONT

Work as for back as far as **. Place markers as for back.

NECK AND RAGLAN SHAPING

First row: K40(44;48) and leave these sts of left front on a spare N, c/off 1, K to end. Cont on 40(44;48) sts now rem on N for right front. Work raglan shapings as given at end of rows on back and **at the same time** for neck shaping dec 1 st at neck edge on every fol 5th(4th;4th) row 12(14;16) times. Note that for the last raglan dec there are insufficient sts to work the normal double dec so replace this by working 2 single decs at neck edge on 2 consecutive rows. C/off rem 2 sts. Rejoin yarn to neck edge of left front sts and complete as for right front rev shapings.

SLEEVES

With 2,75 mm Ns c/on 47(51;53) sts and work in single rib as on back welt for same number of rows. Change to 3 mm Ns and work in patt but inc 1 st at both ends of every fol 10th row 8(8;10) times working extra sts into patt. Cont on 63(67;73) sts until work measures 24(26;29) cm from beg, ending with a 2nd patt row.

RAGLAN SHAPING

Work as given for back and after all rows have been completed c/off rem 11(11;13) sts.

NECKBAND

Sew raglan seams matching markers. With RS of work facing and using 2,75 mm Ns, pick up and K42(45;48) sts up right front neck edge, 10(10;12) sts across sleeve top, 31(35;39) sts across back neck, 10(10;12) sts across left sleeve top and 42(45;48) sts down left front neck. You will need 2 pairs of Ns, picking up sts onto 3 Ns and working with the 4th. Work 1 row in rib beg and ending with K1. Cont in rib but dec 1 st at both ends of next 3 rows. Work 1 row straight then inc 1 st at both ends of next 3 rows. C/off RW.

TO MAKE UP
Join side and sleeve seams. Sew shaped ends of neckband, then fold band in half to wrong side and slip-st cast-off edge to back of picked-up sts.

Child's raglan cardigan

MATERIALS
Confort DK (50 g balls) 5(6;6) balls; one pair each 3 mm and 3,25 mm knitting needles; 3 buttons.

MEASUREMENTS
To fit chest 56(61;66) cm; actual all round measurement 62,5(66;69) cm; length to back neck 32(35;38) cm; sleeve seam 23(25;27) cm.

TENSION
24 sts and 44 rows = 10 cm over Fisherman's Rib using 3,25 mm Ns.

STITCHES USED
Patt st.
First row (right side): K to end.
2nd row: K1, * P1, K1 below; rep from * to last 2 sts, P1, K1. These 2 rows form the patt.

BACK
With 3 mm Ns c/on 75(79;83) sts and work in single rib beg and ending RS rows with P1 and WS rows with K1. Cont until work measures 3,5 cm from beg, ending with a WS row. Change to 3,25 mm Ns and work in patt as given above. Cont until work measures 21(23;25) cm from beg, ending with a 2nd patt row.

RAGLAN SHAPING
Place marker loops of contrasting yarn at each end of last row to indicate beg of armholes. Work 2 rows straight.
3rd row: K3, K3tog, K to last 6 sts, SKTPO, K3.
4th row: As 2nd patt row. Rep last 4 rows 11(12;13) times more. C/off rem 27 sts loosely for back neck.

POCKET LININGS
Make 2 alike. With 3,25 mm Ns c/on 21 sts and work 2 rows in rib as on welt then work in patt until work measures 4 cm from beg, ending with a 2nd patt row. Cut yarn and leave sts on a holder.

RIGHT FRONT
With 3 mm Ns c/on 39(41;43) sts and work in single rib as on back welt for same number of rows. Change to 3,25 mm Ns and work in patt until work measures 7(8;9) cm from beg, ending with 2nd patt row.

POCKET OPENING
Next row: K10(10;12), slip off next 21 sts onto a holder, K sts of one pocket lining, then K rem 8(10;10) sts at side edge. Cont in patt until work measures 21(23;25) cm from beg, ending with a 2nd patt row.

RAGLAN AND FRONT SHAPING
Place marker loop at side edge as for back.
First row: C/off 1 (front shaping), K to end. Work 1 row straight.
3rd row: C/off 1, K to last 6 sts, SKTPO, K3. For **first size** cont to dec 1 st at front edge on next alt row then every fol 4th row 9 times more; (for **2nd** and **3rd sizes** dec 1 st at front edge on every fol 4th row 10 times more). **At the same time** cont to work raglan dec in same position on every fol 4th row 10(11;12) times more. Work 2 rows on rem 5 sts. Now dec 1 st at **front** edge on next 3 rows. C/off rem 2 sts.

LEFT FRONT
Work as for right front, rev position of pocket opening and all shapings.

SLEEVES
Both alike. With 3 mm Ns c/on 43(49;55) sts and work in single rib as on back welt but cont until work measures 5 cm ending with a WS row. Change to 3,25 mm Ns and work in patt but inc 1 st at both ends of every fol 8th row 4(6;8) times then every fol 6th row 6(4;2) times working extra sts into patt. Cont on 63(69;75) sts until work measures 23(25;27) cm from beg, ending with a 2nd patt row.

RAGLAN SHAPING
Work exactly as for back raglan and when all shapings are completed c/off rem 15(17;19) sts.

POCKET BORDERS
Both alike. Slip sts from holder onto 3 mm N, join on yarn with RS facing, inc in first st, [K1, P1] 9 times, K1, inc in last st. [23 sts.]
Next row: P1, * K1, P1; rep from * to end. Cont in rib as now set for a further 2 rows. C/off loosely RW.

FRONT BORDER
First join raglan seams. With 3 mm Ns c/on 9 sts and work in rib.
First row (right side): K2, [P1, K1] 3 times, K1.
2nd row: [K1, P1] 4 times, K1. Work 4 more rows in rib then make buttonhole.
7th row: Rib 4, c/off 2, rib to end. On fol row c/on 2 sts over buttonhole. Cont in rib making 2 more buttonholes each 8(9;10) cm above cast-off edge of previous one then cont until border when slightly stretched fits along right front edge, all round neckline including tops of sleeves and down left front. Leave sts on a safety pin with some yarn attached for adjustment.

TO MAKE UP
Join side and sleeve seams. Slip-st pocket linings in place on WS and neatly sew ends of borders on RS. Pin on front border stretching it slightly around the neckline so that it fits well, replace sts on a 3 mm needle, adjust length if necessary and c/off. Sew on front border as pinned and sew on buttons to correspond with buttonholes.

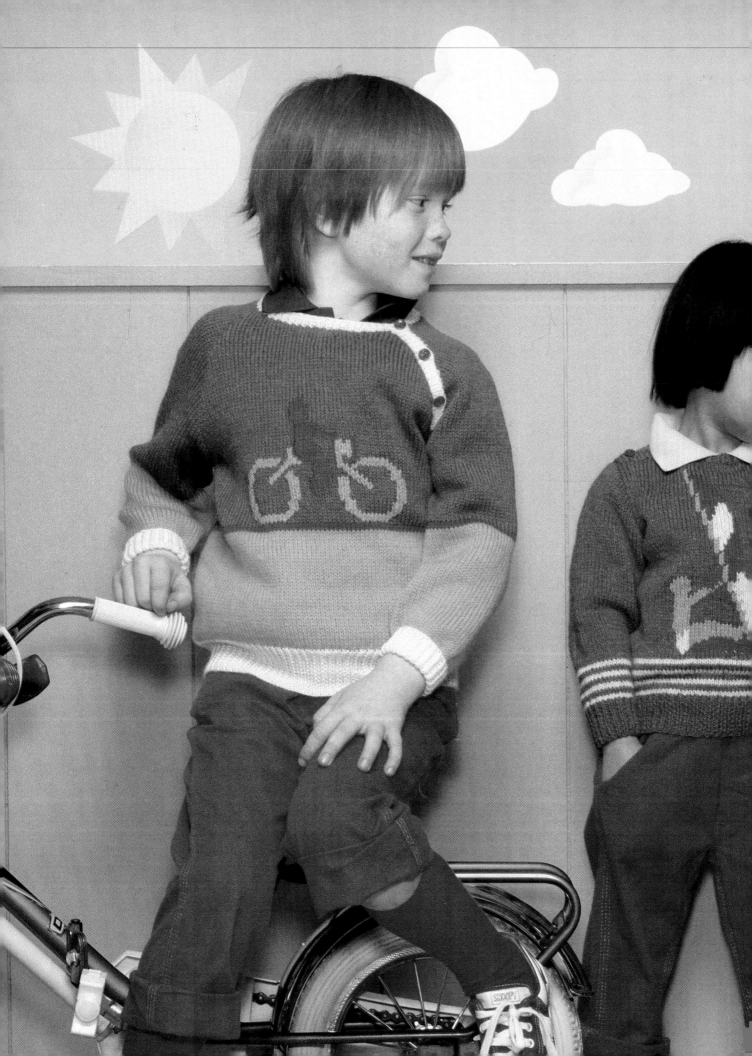

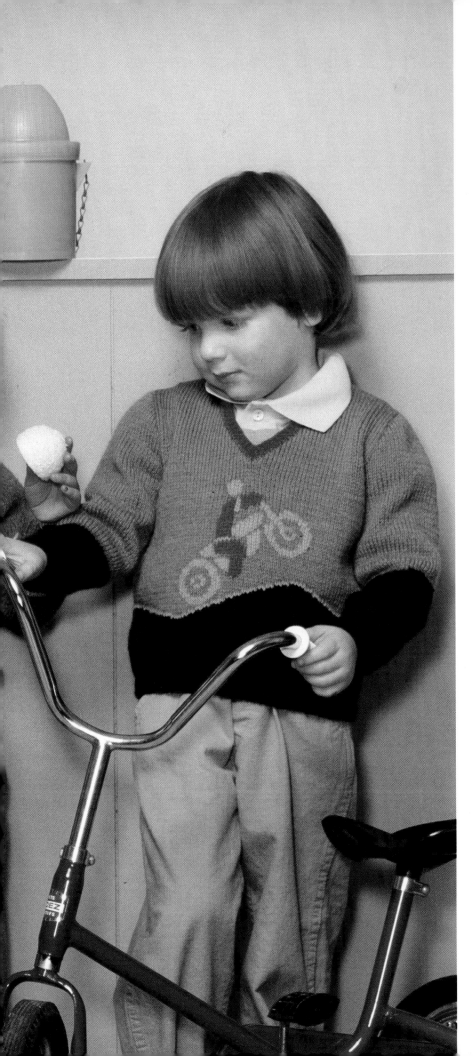

Motion motifs

Bicycle sweater

MATERIALS
Confort DK (50 g balls); 2(2;3) balls Blue (A); 1(2;2) balls Yellow (B); 1 ball each White (C) and Red (D). One pair each 2,75 mm and 3,75 mm knitting needles; 3 buttons.

MEASUREMENTS
To fit chest 56(61;66) cm.

STITCHES USED
Embroidery: Worked in Swiss Darning over the completed knitting.

TENSION
24 sts and 32 rows = 10 cm using stocking stitch and 3,75 mm Ns.

BACK
Using 2,75 mm Ns and C, c/on 76(81;86) sts and work 5(6;6) cm in single rib. Change to 3,75 mm Ns and B, and cont in st st. When work measures 14(16;17) cm, work 2 rows in D, then complete work in A.
When work measures 22(24;26) cm shape armholes: dec 1 st at each end of every alt row 23(25;27) times. C/off rem 30(31;32) sts for neck.

FRONT
Work as given for back. When work measures 22(24;26) cm shape armholes: dec 1 st at each end of every alt row 21(23;25) times. At the same time, when work measures 32(35;38) cm shape neck: c/off centre 10(11;12) sts and cont each side separately, casting off at neck edge on every alt row as fols: 5 sts (once), 3 sts (once), 2 sts (once) and 1 st (once). Fasten off rem 1 st. Complete 2nd side to match, rev all shapings.

LEFT SLEEVE
Using 2,75 mm Ns and C, c/on 40(43;46) sts and work 5(6;6) cm in single rib. Change to 3,75 mm Ns and B and cont in st st, inc 6(8;10) sts evenly across first row. [46(51;56) sts.] Cont by inc 1 st at each end of every 8th row (5 times), then 1 st at each end of every 6th row (3 times) [Inc 1 st at each end of every 8th row (8 times); inc 1 st at each end of every 8th row (8 times).] [62(67;72) sts.]
At the same time, when work measures 17(19;20) cm work 2 rows in D, then complete work in A.
When work measures 25(27;29) cm shape armholes: dec 1 st at beg of

every alt row 23(25;27) times, and **at the same time,** dec 1 st at end (front edge) of every alt row 21(23;25) times, then c/off at front edge on every alt row as fols: 6 sts (3 times) [6 sts (twice), 7 sts (once); 6 sts (once), 7 sts (twice)].

RIGHT SLEEVE
Work as for left sleeve, rev all shapings.

EMBROIDERY
Embroider the motif in Swiss Darning onto the front of the sweater, working from the chart, and beg on the 2nd row of A.

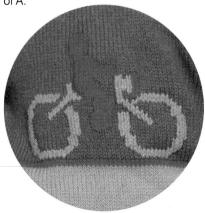

TO MAKE UP
Stitch both back raglan seams and right front raglan seam.

NECK BORDER
Using 2,75 mm Ns and C, pick up and knit approximately 96(100;104) sts around neck and work 5 rows in single rib. C/off.

LEFT ARMHOLE BORDERS
Using 2,75 mm Ns and C, pick up and K38(41;44) sts across the last 13(14; 15) cm at neck edge of the slope of the left front armhole, and work 4 rows in single rib, working 3 buttonholes (2 sts wide) on the 2nd row: the first is worked 8(9;10) sts in from right hand end of work, the others spaced 11(12;13) sts apart. C/off on the 5th row. Work in the same way omitting buttonholes on the sloping edge of the left front armhole on the sleeve.
Stitch left front raglan seam below the borders.
Stitch side and sleeve seams.
Lap the front armhole border over the sleeve border and stitch the lower ends in place.
Sew on buttons.

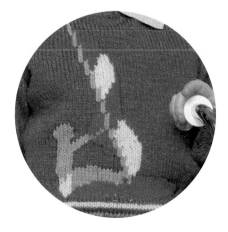

Windsurfer sweater

MATERIALS
Confort DK (50 g balls); 3(4;5) balls Blue (A); 1 ball White (B); 1 ball Red (C) and 1 ball Yellow (D). One pair 3 mm and one pair 3,75 mm knitting needles; 4 buttons.

MEASUREMENTS
To fit chest 56(61;66) cm.

STITCHES USED
Embroidery: Worked in Swiss Darning after the knitting is complete.

TENSION
24 sts and 32 rows = 10 cm using stocking stitch and 3,75 mm Ns.

BACK
Using 3 mm Ns and A, c/on 74(82;86) sts and work 4 cm in single rib. Change to 3,75 mm Ns and cont in st st as fols: * 2 rows in B, 2 rows in A *: rep from * to * 4 times in all, then complete work in A. When work measures 22(24;26) cm **shape armholes:** ** c/off 3 sts at the beg of next 2 rows, then 2 sts at the beg of next 2 rows, then 1 st at the beg of next 6(8;10) rows. [58(64;66) sts.] ** When work measures 33(36;39) cm **shape shoulders and neck:** c/off 8(9;9) sts at the beg of next row, then c/off centre 16(18;20) sts for neck on the same row, work to end of row. Cont on this side only. C/off 8(9;9) sts at the beg of next row. *** C/off 5 sts at the beg of next row (neck shaping). C/off rem 8(9;9) sts at the beg of next row. *** Complete other side from *** to ***, rev all shapings.

FRONT
Work as given for back.
When work measures 22(24;26) cm

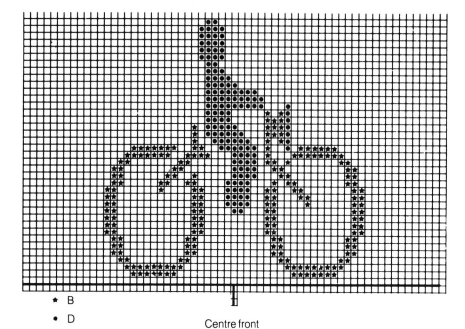

• B

• D

Centre front

work the same shapings for armholes as given for back from ** to **.

When work measures 30(33;36) cm **shape neck:** c/off centre 12(14;16) sts and cont each side separately, casting off at neck edge on every alt row as fols: 3 sts (once), 2 sts (once), 1 st (twice). When work measures 32(35;38) cm **shape shoulders:** c/off 8(9;9) sts on side edge at beg of next row. Work 1 row, then c/off rem 8(9;9) sts. Complete 2nd side to match, rev all shapings.

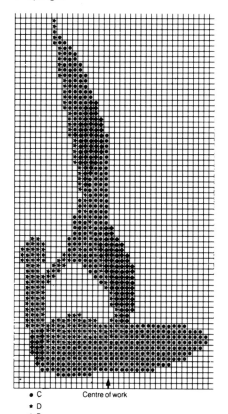

- • C
- ★ D
- ◆ B

Centre of work

SLEEVES
Using 3 mm Ns and A, c/on 40(44;46) sts and work 4 cm in single rib, inc 4(6;8) sts evenly across last row. [44(50;54) sts.]

Change to 3,75 mm Ns and cont in the same stripe pattern as for back and front, then complete work in A. **At the same time**, inc 1 st at each end of every 8th row (6 times). [56(62;66) sts.]

When work measures 23(25;27) cm **shape armholes:** c/off 3 sts at the beg of next 2 rows then * 2 sts at the beg of next 4 rows, then 1 st at the beg of next 2 rows *: rep from * to * 3 times in all; then c/off 2 sts at the beg of next 0(2;4) rows, then 3 sts at the beg of next 4 rows. C/off rem 8(10;10) sts.

EMBROIDERY
Embroider the motif onto the completed front using Swiss Darning and working from the chart, beginning on 2nd row of A after last stripe of B.

NECK AND SHOULDER BORDERS
Using 3 mm Ns and A, pick up and K16(18;18) sts across the left front shoulder, then 30(32;34) sts around front neck, then 16(18;18) sts across the right front shoulder. Work 5 rows in single rib, working twice into 1 st on each side of neck on the first row to form a corner. On the 3rd row, work 2 buttonholes (2 sts wide) on each shoulder: the first is worked 1 st in from the corner at neck, the 2nd is worked 7 sts from the first. C/off on the 6th row. Pick up and K16(18;18) sts across the right back shoulder, then 22(24;26) sts across back neck, then 16(18;18) sts across the left back shoulder. Work in the same way as given for front, omitting buttonholes.

TO MAKE UP
Tack the shoulder borders at outer edge, lapping the front border over the back border.
Stitch side seams.
Stitch sleeve seams. Sew in sleeves.
Sew on buttons.

Highrider pullover

MATERIALS
Confort DK (50 g balls); 1(2;2) balls Navy (A); 3(3;4) balls Blue (B); 1 ball each Red (C) and Yellow (D). One pair each 3 mm and 3,75 mm knitting needles; 1 set of 4 x 3 mm double-pointed needles.

MEASUREMENTS
To fit chest 56(61;66) cm.

STITCHES USED
Fair Isle stocking stitch: Work from the chart.
Motif: Worked in Swiss Darning over the completed knitting.

TENSION
24 sts and 32 rows = 10 cm using stocking stitch and 3,75 mm Ns.

BACK
* Using 3 mm Ns and A, c/on 76(82;86) sts and work 4 cm in single rib. Change to 3,75 mm Ns and cont in st st, working from the chart, and making sure you twist yarns on wrong side of work at each colour change, then complete work in st st using B.

When work measures 22(24;26) cm **shape armholes:** c/off 3 sts at beg of next 2 rows, then 2 sts at the beg of next 4 rows, then 1 st at the beg of next 4(6;8) rows. [58(62;64) sts rem.] *

When work measures 33(36;39) cm **shape shoulders:** c/off 5 sts at the beg of next 6 rows (c/off 5 sts at the beg of next 4 rows, then 6 sts at the beg of next 2 rows; c/off 5 sts at the beg of next 2 rows, then 6 sts at the beg of next 4 rows.) C/off rem 28(30;30) sts.

FRONT
Begin work as given for back from * to *, working from the appropriate chart for the Fair Isle. **At the same time**, shape neck: divide work into 2 equal sections and cont each side separately, dec 1 st at neck edge on every alt row (10 times), then dec 1 st at neck edge on every 3rd row (4 times) then dec 1 st at neck edge on next alt row for sizes 2 and 3 only.

When work measures 33(36;39) cm **shape shoulders:** c/off 5 sts at beg of next 2 alt rows (c/off 5 sts at beg of next 2 alt rows; c/off 5 sts at beg of next alt row, then 6 sts at beg of next alt row). Work 1 row then c/off rem 5(6;6) sts. Complete other side to match, rev all shapings.

RIGHT SLEEVE
Using 3 mm Ns and A, c/on 38(44;48) sts and work 4 cm in single rib, then change to 3,75 mm Ns and cont in Fair Isle st st, working from the chart; and inc 4 sts evenly across first row [42(48;52) sts], then complete work in st st, using B.

Cont by inc 1 st at each end of every 8th row (7 times). [56(62;66) sts.]

When work measures 26(28;30) cm **shape armholes:** c/off 3 sts at the beg of next 2 rows, then 2 sts at the beg of next 6 rows, then 1 st at the beg of next 8(12;16) rows, then 3 sts at the beg of next 2 rows, then 4 sts at the beg of next 4 rows. C/off rem 8(10;10) sts.

LEFT SLEEVE
Work as for right sleeve, working from the corresponding chart.

EMBROIDERY
Embroider the motif in Swiss Darning onto the completed front, working from the chart, and beg on the 3rd row of colour B.
Using D, embroider a row of Swiss Darning on the first row of colour B on the front and back. Work in the same way on the sleeves, using colour C.

TO MAKE UP
Stitch shoulder seams

NECK BORDER
Using the set of 4 x 3 mm Ns and C, beginning at centre front, pick up and K approximately 40(42;44) sts along the right front neck edge, then 26(28;28) sts around back neck, then 40(42;44) sts along the left front neck edge. Work 5 rows (not rounds) of single rib, dec 1 st at each end of every row. C/off.
Stitch neck border seam into a point.
Stitch side seams.
Stitch sleeve seams. Sew in sleeves.

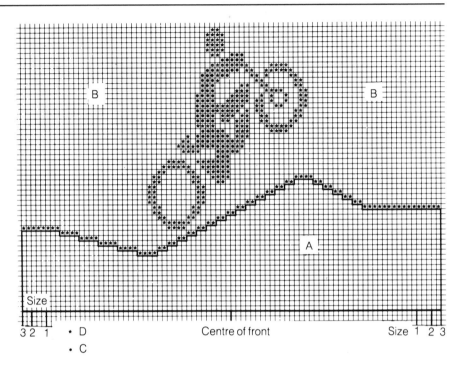

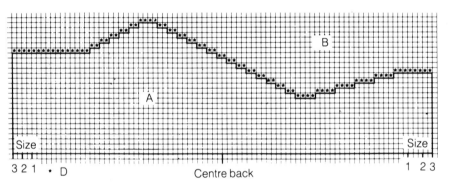

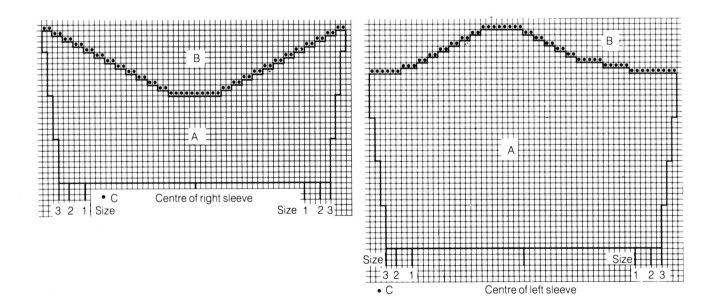

Sweater, coat and hat

MATERIALS
Corrida 4 (50 g balls); **Sweater:** 4(5;6) balls White (A); 1 ball per size Red (B); **Coat:** 4 Pingouin 8(9;10); **Hat:** 2 balls. One pair each 3 mm, 3,25 mm and 4 mm knitting needles; 3,25 mm circular knitting needle; 3 buttons for sweater; 6 buttons for coat.

MEASUREMENTS
Sweater: To fit chest 56(61;66) cm; actual all round measurement 60(66; 72) cm; length to underarm 18(20;22) cm; sleeve seam 23(25;27) cm.
Coat: To fit chest 56(61;66) cm; actual all round measurement (as worn) 62(67;72) cm; length to shoulder 41 (44;47) cm; sleeve seam 27(29;31) cm.

TENSION
Sweater: 20 sts and 34 rows = 10 cm over patt st, using 4 mm Ns.
Coat: 24 sts and 28 rows = 10 cm over patt st, using 4 mm Ns.

Raglan sweater

STITCHES USED
Moss Stitch (mst) worked on an even number of sts as fols:
First row (right side): * K1, P1; rep from * to end.
2nd row: * P1, K1; rep from * to end.
These 2 rows form mst patt.

BACK
Using 3 mm Ns and A, c/on 60(66;72) sts and work 4(4;5) cm K1, P1 rib. Change to 4 mm Ns and beg with a K row work in st st, working 6(8;8) rows in B, 6 rows in A, 6(8;8) rows in B. Now using A, K 1 row on RS, then beg with a 2nd patt row cont in mst until work measures 18(20;22) cm from beg, ending with a WS row. V.

SHAPE RAGLAN
** C/off 2 sts at beg of next 2 rows. (For large size only, work 3 rows straight then dec at each end of fol row.) Now dec 1 st at each end of next 5(6;6) WS rows. Cont to dec at each end of every alt row and **at the same time** change to B and K 1 row on RS, then K 1 row on WS, then work 6 rows st st in A and 6(8;8) rows st st in B. ** Cont in st st using A and dec 1 st at each end of next 7(7;8) alt rows. C/off rem 18(20;22) sts for back neck.

FRONT
Work as for back until 32(34;36) sts rem, ending with a WS row.

SHAPE NECK
First row: K13 and leaves these sts of left front on a spare N. C/off next 6(8;10) sts, K to end. Cont on 13 sts rem on N for right front and work 1 row.
*** C/off 2 sts at beg of next and fol alt row, then 1 st at beg of fol 2 alt rows and **at the same time**, dec 1 st at raglan edge on every WS row 5 times. C/off rem 2 sts. Rejoin yarn to neck edge of left front sts and complete as for right front from *** to end.
Note: front is 4 rows shorter than back.

RIGHT SLEEVE
Using 3 mm Ns and A, c/on 30(34;36) sts and work 4(4;5) cm K1, P1 rib, inc 10(10;12) sts evenly across last row. [40(44;48) sts.] Change to 4 mm Ns and beg with a first patt row cont in mst, inc 1 st at each end of every fol 10th (12th; 12th) row 5 times. [50(54; 58) sts.] Cont straight until work measures 23(25;27) cm from beg, ending with a WS row. V.

SHAPE RAGLAN
Work as for back raglan from ** to **. Cont in st st using A and dec 1 st at each end of next 5(5;6) alt rows. [Ending with a P row and 12 sts rem.] For front edge of sleeve c/off 3 sts at beg of next 2 RS rows and for back edge of sleeve dec 1 st at beg of next 2 WS rows. C/off rem 4 sts.

LEFT SLEEVE
Work as for right sleeve rev top shaping on last 4 rows.

MAKE UP AND BORDERS
Stitch back raglan seams and right front seam matching stripes. With RS facing and using 3 mm Ns and A, pick up and K65(69;73) sts all around neck edge. Work 3 rows K1, P1 rib. C/off loosely RW. Using 3 mm Ns and A, beg at the 2 rows worked in B at end of mst section, pick up and K25(27;29) sts along left raglan edge of front. Rib 1 row, then make buttonholes.
Next row: Rib 3, c/off 2, [rib until there are 7(8;9) sts on right N after previous buttonhole, c/off 2 sts] twice, rib to end. On fol row c/on 2 sts over each buttonhole. C/off RW. Work similar border on corresponding edge of left sleeve omitting buttonholes.
Stitch left raglan seam below borders and catch edges of borders in place.
Stitch side and sleeve seams matching stripes. Sew on buttons.
DO NOT IRON.

Hat
Using 3,25 mm Ns, c/on 100 sts and work 21 cm K1, P1 rib. Shape top:
First row: K1, P1 [K3tog, P1] 24 times, K1, P1. [52 sts.] Work 5 rows straight.
7th row: [K1, P3tog] 13 times. Work 4 rows on rem 26 sts then cut yarn, thread through rem sts, draw up tightly and sew securely, then stitch seam rev it at lower edge on depth required for brim.

Coat

STITCHES USED
Patt st is a combination of Irish moss st (IM) and rev st st, worked over a multiple of 7 sts plus 5 as fols:
First row (right side): For IM [K1, P1] twice, K1, * P2, then for IM [K1, P1] twice, K1;*
2nd row: For IM [P1, K1] twice, P1, * K2, then for IM [P1, K1] twice, P1.*
3rd row: [P1, K1] twice, P1, * P2, then [P1, K1] twice, P1.*
4th row: [K1, P1] twice, K1, * K2, then [K1, P1] twice, K1.*
These 4 rows form patt.

BACK

Using 3,25 mm Ns, c/on 74(80;86) sts and work in K1, P1 rib for 4 rows inc 1 st in centre of last row. [75 (81;87) sts.] Change to 4 mm Ns and patt as fols:
First size: Work first row in patt as above. **2nd size:** K1, P2, then for IM [K1, P1] twice, K1, then rep from * to * in first patt row, P2, K1. **3rd size:** For IM [P1, K1] twice, P2, [K1, P1] twice, K1, then rep from * to * in first patt row ending last rep with 4 sts in IM. Cont in patt as now set working **first size** as given above (for **2nd size** 1 st in IM at each end; for **3rd size** 4 sts in IM at each end.) Cont until work measures 27(29;31) cm from beg, ending with a WS row. V.

SHAPE ARMHOLES

C/off 2 sts at beg of next 6 rows and 1 st at beg of fol 6(8;10) rows. Cont on rem 57(61;65) sts until work measures 41(44;47) cm from beg, ending with a WS row.

SHAPE SHOULDERS

C/off 5(6;6) sts at beg of next 4 rows and 7(6;8) sts at beg of fol 2 rows. C/off rem 23(25;25) sts for back neck.

POCKET LININGS

Make 2 alike. Using 4 mm Ns, c/on 26 sts and work in patt as given above for 22(24;26) rows. Cut yarn and leave sts on a holder.

RIGHT FRONT

Using 3,25 mm Ns, c/on 46(50;52) sts and work 4 rows K1, P1 rib inc 1 st in centre of last row for first and 3rd sizes only. [47(50;53) sts.] Change to 4 mm Ns and patt.
First row: Work as for first patt row to last 0(3;6) sts (for **2nd size** P2, K1; for **3rd size** P2, work 4 sts in IM). Cont as now set until 22(24;26) rows in patt have been worked.

POCKET OPENING

Patt 14(14;21) sts, sl next 26 sts onto a holder, work in patt across sts of one pocket lining, patt rem 7(10;6) sts at side edge. Cont in patt until work measures 11(12;13) cm from beg, ending with a WS row.
Next row (buttonholes): Work 1 st, c/off 2, work until there are 9 sts on right N after previous buttonhole, c/off 2, work to end. On fol row c/on 2 sts over each buttonhole. Make 2 more pairs of buttonholes each 7(7,5;8) cm above cast-off edge of previous pair. After completing last pair of buttonholes, shape front: dec 1 st at beg of next row and fol 20(21;21) alt rows. **At the same time** keep side edge straight until work matches back to armhole ending with RS row.

SHAPE ARMHOLE

C/off 2 sts at beg of next and fol 2 alt rows and 1 st at same edge on next 3(4;5) alt rows. Now keep this edge straight until work matches back to shoulder ending at side edge.

SHAPE SHOULDER

C/off 5(6;6) sts at beg of next and fol alt row. Work 1 row then c/off rem 7(6;8) sts.

LEFT FRONT

Work as for right front rev arrangement of patt, pocket and all shapings, and omitting buttonholes.

SLEEVES

Using 3,25 mm Ns, c/on 42(46;50) sts and work in K1, P1 rib for 4 rows inc 5 sts evenly across last row. [47(51;55) sts.] Change to 4 mm Ns and patt first row: **First size:** Work patt rows as given above. **2nd size:** P2, then work as for first patt row ending P2. **3rd size:** For IM P1, K1, then P2, then work as for first patt row ending P2, then for IM K1, P1. For all sizes cont as now set inc 1 st at each end of every fol 6th(6th;7th) row 11 times working extra sts into patt. Cont on 69(73;77) sts until work measures 27(29;31) cm from beg, ending with a WS row. V.

SHAPE SLEEVE TOP

C/off 2 sts at beg of next 6 rows, 1 st at beg of fol 6(8;10) rows, 2 sts at beg of next 10(12;12) rows and 4 sts at beg of fol 4 rows. C/off rem 15(13;15) sts.

POCKET BORDERS

Using 3,25 mm Ns, pick up sts from holder with RS facing for first row and K 1 row working 3 inc. [29 sts.] Work 3 rows K1, P1 rib. C/off loosely RW.

FRONT BORDER

Stitch shoulder seams.
With RS facing and using 3,25 mm circular N pick up and K65(70;75) sts along straight front edge of right front, 45(48;50) sts along slope, 23(25;25) sts across back neck, 45(48;50) sts down left front slope and 65(70;75) sts along straight front edge. [243(261;275) sts.] Work 3 rows K1, P1 rib. C/off loosely RW.

TO MAKE UP

Set in sleeves then stitch side and sleeve seams. Slip-stitch pocket linings in place on WS then neatly sew ends of borders on RS. Sew on buttons.
DO NOT IRON.

Sporting togs

MATERIALS
Sleeveless jacket: Confort (50 g balls); 2(3;3) balls each Grey (A) and Red (B); 1 ball each per size Yellow (C) and Blue (D); **Sweater:** Confort (50 g balls); 2(3;3) balls Grey (A); 1 ball each per size Blue (B); Yellow (C) and Red (D); 1 pair each 3 mm, 3,25 mm, 4 mm and 5 mm knitting needles; 5 hooks and eyes for jacket and 2 buttons for sweater.

MEASUREMENTS
Sleeveless jacket: to fit chest 56(61; 66) cm; actual all round measurement 62(67;72) cm; length to shoulder 36(40;43) cm.
Sweater: to fit chest 56(61;66) cm; actual all round measurement 60(65;70) cm; length to shoulder 34(37;40) cm; sleeve seam 28(30;32) cm.

TENSION
Sleeveless Jacket: 17 sts and 23 rows = 10 cm using st st and 5 mm Ns.
Sweater: 24 sts and 30 rows = 10 cm using st st and 3,25 mm Ns.

Sleeveless jacket
BACK
Using 4 mm Ns and A, c/on 53(57;61) sts and work 4 cm K1, P1 rib, ending with a WS row. Change to 5 mm Ns and cont in st st until work measures 22(25;27) cm from beg, ending with a P row.

SHAPE ARMHOLE
C/off 2(2;3) sts at beg of next 2 rows and 1 st at beg of fol 2(4;4) rows. Cont on rem 47(49;51) sts until work measures 36(40;43) cm from beg, ending with a P row.

SHAPE SHOULDERS AND NECK
First row: C/off 7(8;8) sts, K until there are 9 sts on right N, leave these for right back, c/off 15(15;17) sts, K to end. Cont on 16(17;17) sts rem at end of N for left back. C/off 7(8;8) sts at beg of next row and 2 sts at neck edge on fol row. C/off rem 7 sts. Rejoin yarn to neck edge of rem sts, c/off 2, P to end. C/off rem 7 sts.

LEFT FRONT
First work pocket lining: C/on 12(13;14) sts using 5 mm Ns and B. Beg with a K row and work 4(6;8) rows in st st then cut yarn and leave sts on a holder. ** For main part, using 4 mm Ns and B, c/on 26(28;30) sts. Work in rib as on back welt for same number of rows,

then change to 5 mm Ns and beg with a K row, work 4(6;8) rows in st st.**

POCKET OPENING
First row: K14(15;16) sts then onto same N K sts of pocket lining, turn, leaving rem 12(13;14) sts of front section unworked. Cont on sts of side section and pocket lining for a further 19 rows thus ending at side edge after a P row.
21st row: K14(15;16) sts, then c/off rem 12(13;14) sts of pocket lining and fasten off. With RS facing rejoin yarn to 12(13;14) sts of front section which were left unworked on first row, K to end. Work a further 20 rows on these sts.
42nd row: P12(13;14) then P14(15;16) sts of side section. *** Cont in st st across all sts until work measures 22(25;27) cm from beg, ending with a P row.

SHAPE ARMHOLES
C/off 2(2;3) sts at beg of next row and 1 st on next 1(2;2) alt rows. Cont on rem 23(24;25) sts until 9 rows less have been worked than on back to beg of shoulder, thus ending at front edge.

SHAPE NECK AND SHOULDERS
C/off 4(4;5) sts at beg of next row, 2 sts at same edge on fol alt row and 1 st on next 3 alt rows. For shoulder c/off 7(8;8) sts at beg of next row, work 1 row, then c/off rem 7 sts.

RIGHT FRONT
Beg with main part work as for left front from ** to **

POCKET OPENING
First row: K12(13;14), turn and cont on these sts for front section leaving sts of side section unworked. Cont on front section for a further 20 rows thus ending at the opening after a K row. Cut yarn. Now work pocket lining as for left front but after working 4(6;8) rows do not cut yarn.
Next row: K these sts, then onto same N K14(15;16) sts of side section which were left unworked at beg of pocket opening. Work a further 19 rows on these sts.
21st row: C/off 12(13;14) sts, K to end. On fol row rejoin the 2 groups of sts. Complete as for left front from *** to end rev all shapings.

ARMHOLE BORDERS
Make 2. Using 4 mm Ns and C, c/on 39(45;51) sts and work in rib as on welt

but after working first row shape sides by c/on 7 sts at beg of next 4 rows and 6 sts at beg of fol 6 rows, working extra sts into rib. Cont in rib on 103(109;115) sts until work measures 5 cm measured at centre ending with WS row. Now c/off 6 sts at beg of next 6 rows and 7 sts at beg of fol 4 rows. C/off rem 39(45;51) sts.

COLLAR
Using 4 mm Ns and D, c/on 41(41;45) sts and work in rib as on welt but after working first row, c/on 5 sts at beg of next 12 rows and 4 sts at beg of fol 2 rows. Cont on these 109(109;113) sts until work measures 6 cm measured at centre, ending with a RS row. C/off 4 sts at beg of next 2 rows and 5 sts at beg of fol 12 rows. C/off rem 41(41; 45) sts.

RIGHT FRONT BORDER
Using 4 mm Ns and B, c/on 8 sts.
First row: Sl 1 KW [K1, P1] 3 times, K1. Rep this row until work measures 32(36;39) cm from beg. C/off.

LEFT FRONT BORDER
Rib is worked as fols:
First row: Sl 1 PW [K1, P1] 3 times, K1. Rep this row until border is same length as right front border. C/off.

POCKET BORDERS
With RS facing and using 4 mm Ns and B, pick up and K19 sts along side edge of front section on left front pocket opening. Work in rib as on welt for 3 rows. C/off RW. Work similar border on right front pocket.

TO MAKE UP
First work the initial in Swiss Darning on left front using D, placing lower edge of

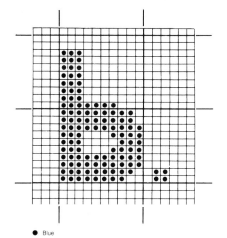

● Blue

motif in line with beg of armhole shaping and with the front edge of motif 4 cm from front edge of st st. Stitch shoulder seams. Stitch front borders into position. With right sides tog stitch cast-on edges of collar around neck edges leaving half the width of front borders free. Fold collar in half to WS and slip-st cast-off edges to previous seam. With right sides tog stitch shaped edge of armhole borders to armhole edges. Stitch side seams and ends of borders. Complete borders as for collar. Slip-st pocket linings in place on WS and neatly stitch ends of borders on RS. Sew on the hooks and eyes placing the first at 3(3;4) cm from beg and 4 more at intervals of 7(8;8,5) cm measuring from centres.

Striped sweater

Stripe sequence is worked as fols: working in st st work * 8 rows in A, 8 rows in C, 8 rows in A, 8 rows in D, 8 rows in A, 8 rows in B.* Rep from * to * throughout.

BACK

Using 3 mm Ns and A, c/on 72(78;84) sts and work 5(6;6) cm K1, P1 rib. Change to 3,25 mm Ns and beg with a K row cont in striped st st as above until work measures 23(25;27) cm from beg, ending with a P row.

SHAPE ARMHOLES

C/off 3 sts at beg of next 2 rows, 2 sts at beg of fol 4 rows and 1 st at beg of next 2(4;6) rows. Cont on rem 56(60;64) sts until work measures 34(37;40) cm from beg, ending with a P row.

SHAPE SHOULDERS AND NECK

C/off 5(6;6) sts at beg of next 2 rows.
3rd row: C/off 5(6;6) sts, K until there

are 8(8;10) sts on right N, leave these for right back, c/off next 20 sts, K to end. Cont on 13(14;16) sts rem at end of N for left back. C/off 5(6;6) sts at beg of next row and 3 sts at neck edge of fol row. C/off rem 5(5;7) sts. Rejoin yarn to neck edge of rem sts, c/off 3, P to end. C/off rem 5(5;7) sts.

FRONT

Work as for back until 14 rows less have been worked than on back to beg of shoulder shaping, thus ending with a P row.

SHAPE NECK AND SHOULDERS

First row: K23(25;27) and leave these sts of left front on a spare N, c/off next 10 sts, K to end. Cont on 23(25;27) sts now rem on N for right front and P 1 row. ** C/off 3 sts at beg of next row, 2 sts at same edge on fol alt row and 1 st on next 3 alt rows. ** Work 2 rows straight thus ending at side. For shoulder c/off 5(6;6) sts at beg of next and fol alt row. Work 1 row then c/off rem 5(5;7) sts. Rejoin yarn to neck edge of left front sts. Cont as for right front from ** to **. Now work shoulder shaping as for right front. Note this shoulder is lower than right front to allow for border.

SLEEVES

Using 3 mm Ns and A, c/on 36(38;40) sts and work 5(6;6) cm K1, P1 rib, inc 3(5;7) sts evenly across last row. [39(43;47) sts.] Change to 3,25 mm Ns and beg with a K row cont in st st, working 8 rows in A, 8 rows in B, then in striped patt as given above. **At the same time** inc 1 st at each end of every 8th row 7(7;8) times. Cont on these 53(57;63) sts until you have worked 16 more rows than on back to beg of armhole, thus ending at same position on striped patt.

SHAPE SLEEVE TOP

C/off 3 sts at beg of next 2 rows, 2 sts at beg of fol 4 rows, 1 st at beg of next 8(8;10) rows, 2 sts at beg of fol 2(4;6) rows, 3 sts at beg of next 2 rows and 4 sts at beg of fol 2 rows. C/off rem 13 sts.

MAKE UP AND BORDERS

Stitch right shoulder seam. With RS facing and using 3 mm Ns and A, pick up and K72 sts all around neck edge. Work in K1, P1 rib for 5 rows. C/off RW. Using 3 mm Ns and A, pick up and K22(24;26) sts along left front shoulder including edge of neckband. Work in

K1, P1 rib for 2 rows then make buttonholes.
3rd row (beg at neck): Rib 2, c/off 1, rib until there are 10 sts on right N after previous buttonhole. C/off 1, rib to end. On fol row, c/on 1 st over each buttonhole. Rib 1 row. C/off RW: Work similar border on left back shoulder but working only 3 rows in rib and omitting buttonholes.
Lap left front shoulder border over back border and oversew along side edges.
Set in sleeves, stitch side and sleeve seams matching stripes. Sew on buttons.
DO NOT IRON.

Tracksuit top

MATERIALS

Confort (50 g balls); 5(7;8) balls Grey (A); 3(4;5) balls Red (B); 1 pair each 2,75 mm and 3,25 mm knitting needles; narrow elastic for trousers.

MEASUREMENTS

To fit chest 56(61;66) cm; actual all round measurement 63(68;73) cm; length to back neck 35(38;41,5) cm; sleeve seam 24(26;28) cm.

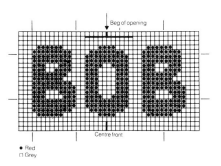

TENSION

24 sts and 30 rows = 10 cm using st st and 3,25 mm Ns.

STITCHES USED

The name is embroidered onto the front afterwards by the method known as Swiss Darning.

BACK

With 2,75 mm Ns and A, c/on 76(82;88) sts and work in single rib for 4 cm. Change to 3,25 mm Ns and work in st st. Cont until work measures 22 (24;26) cm from beg, ending with a P row.**

SHAPE RAGLAN

C/off 3 sts at beg of next 2 rows. Dec 1 st at both ends of next 2 rows, work 1 row then dec at both ends of fol row. Rep last 4 rows 5 times more. Now dec 1 st at both ends of next 6(8;10) alt rows. Cut yarn and leave rem 22(24;26) sts on a holder.

FRONT

Work as for back as far as **.

RAGLAN SHAPING AND FRONT OPENING

First row: C/off 3, K until there are 35(38;41) sts on right N, turn and cont on these sts for left front, leaving rem sts on a spare N. Work 1 row straight. *** Dec 1 st at raglan edge on next 2 rows, work 1 row then dec 1 st at same edge on fol row. Rep last 4 rows 5 times more. Now dec 1 st at same edge on every alt row 3(5;7) times. Cut yarn and leave rem 14(15;16) sts on a holder. With RS facing rejoin yarn to 38(41;44) sts of right front, K to end. C/off 3 sts at beg of fol row. Now complete as for left front from *** to end rev all shapings.

RIGHT SLEEVE

With 2,75 mm Ns and B, c/on 36(40;44) sts and work in single rib for 4 cm working 4(6;8) incs evenly spaced along last row. [40(46;52) sts.] Change to 3,25 mm Ns and work in st st but inc 1 st at both ends of every fol 5th(5th;6th)

row 11 times. Cont on 62(68;74) sts until work measures 24(26;28) cm from beg, ending with a P row.

SHAPE RAGLAN

C/off 3 sts at beg of next 2 rows. Dec 1 st at both ends of next 2 rows, work 1 row then dec 1 st at both ends of fol row. Rep last 4 rows 5 times more. Now dec 1 st at both ends of next 3(5;7) alt rows. You have ended with a P row. [14(16;18) sts rem.] Shape top thus: c/off 3(3;4) sts at beg of next row and next 2 alt rows and at same time dec 1 st at beg of every P row 3 times. C/off rem 2(4;3) sts.

LEFT SLEEVE

Work as for right sleeve but rev shapings on the last 6 rows.

FRONT FACING

With 3,25 mm Ns and B, c/on 4 sts.
1st row: K.
2nd row: Inc in first st, P2, inc in last st.
3rd row: K.
4th row: Inc in first st, P2, turn and cont on these sts to form front opening, leaving rem 3 sts on a holder. Cont in st st and inc at outer edge on every alt row 10 times more, then at same edge on every fol 4th row 2(3;4) times. Work 3 rows straight thus ending at shaped edge. C/off 2 sts at beg of fol row. Cut yarn and leave rem 14(15;16) sts on a holder.
With WS facing rejoin yarn to sts at other side of opening, P2, inc in last st. Cont as for first side rev shaping and after the last inc row work 2 rows straight, c/off 2 sts at beg of fol row then P 1 row on rem 14(15;16) sts. Leave these on a holder.

TO MAKE UP

Join raglan seams. Pin facing to front with K sides tog and sew along sides of opening, then turn facing to inside. Join side and sleeve seams.

HOOD

With RS of work facing and using 3,25 mm Ns and B, K first st of right front tog with first st of this section of

facing. [K next st of front tog with next st of facing] 13(14;15) times, then pick up and K11(13;15) sts across cast-off edges at top of right sleeve, K sts of back, pick up and K11(13;15) sts across cast-off edges of left sleeve then K sts of left front tog with those of this section of facing. Beg with a P row work in st st c/on 4 sts at beg of next 2 rows for hem, then P 1 row straight. [80(88;96) sts.]
5th row: K5(9;8), * inc in next st, K2, inc in next st, K2(2;3); rep from * 11 times more, K rem 3(7;4) sts. Cont on 104 (112;120) sts until work measures 24(26;28) cm from beg of hood. Divide sts onto 2 Ns and holding them with P side inside graft the sts. Alternatively hold them with K side inside and c/off both sets tog. Fold 4 sts along front edge to inside forming hem and slip-stitch in place. Make a long cord using B and thread it through hem to tie under chin. Sew a pompon made in B to each end of cord.
Note: this cord being around the front edge is quite safe. Embroider the name just under front opening using the method known as Swiss Darning.

Jacket

MATERIALS
Confort DK (50 g balls); 7(8;9) balls Red (A) and 1 ball White (B). One pair each 3,25 mm and 4 mm knitting needles; 6 buttons.

MEASUREMENTS
To fit bust/chest 66-71(76-81;87) cm.

STITCHES USED
Fair Isle stocking stitch or embroidery: Work from the chart.

TENSION
22 sts and 28 rows = 10 cm using stocking stitch and 4 mm Ns.

BACK
Using 3,25 mm Ns and A, c/on 77(83;89) sts and work 6 cm in single rib. Change to 4 mm Ns and cont in st st, inc 9(12;15) sts evenly across first row. [86(95;104) sts.] If you choose to work the Fair Isle, work the motifs when work measures 24(28;33) cm leaving 2 sts between each motif, and working 1 motif on each side of the centre 2 sts for sizes 1 and 3, and 1 motif over the centre 15 sts for size 2. (Begin a motif at each end, which will be completed on the front.)
When work measures 29(33;38) cm, shape armholes: c/off 3 sts at the beg of next 2 rows, then 2 sts at the beg of next 2 rows, then 1 st at the beg of next 4(6;8) rows. [72(79;86) sts.]
When work measures 44(50;57) cm, shape shoulders: c/off 7(8;8) sts at the beg of next 2 rows. Next row: c/off 7(8;8) sts at the beg of row, then c/off centre 30(33;36) sts for neck on the same row, work to end. Cont on this side only. C/off 7(8;8) sts at the beg of next row, then 7(7;9) sts at the beg of fol alt row. Complete other side to match, rev all shapings.

RIGHT FRONT
Using 3,25 mm Ns and A, c/on 39(43;47) sts and work 6 cm in single rib. Change to 4 mm Ns and cont in st st, inc 6 sts evenly across first row. [45(49;53) sts.] When work measures 12(14;16) cm work pocket opening: place 25(27;27) sts, 17(19;21) sts in from centre front edge onto a spare N.

Pocket lining (worked separately): Using 4 mm Ns, c/on 25(27;27) sts and work 6(8;10) cm in st st. Place these sts behind the front in place of the sts left on spare N, and cont across all these sts. If you have chosen to work the Fair Isle, begin the motifs when work measures 24(28;33) cm working the first motif 2 sts in from centre front edge.
When work measures 29(33;38) cm shape armholes as fols: with WS facing, c/off 3 sts, then 2 sts at the beg of the next alt row, then 1 st at beg of next 2(3;4) alt rows.
When work measures 31(36;41) cm shape neck: dec 1 st at neck edge on every alt row 2(3;4) times, then * 1 st on next 4th row, 1 st on fol alt row *: rep from * to * 7 times in all. When work measures 44(50;57) cm shape shoulder: c/off at armhole edge on every alt row as fols: 7 sts (twice) and 8 sts (once); 8 sts (3 times); 8 sts (once) and 9 sts (twice).
Using 3,25 mm Ns, rejoin yarn to the sts left at pocket opening. Inc 1 st at each end of first row. [27(29;29) sts.] Work 7 rows in single rib, then c/off.

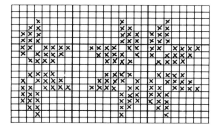

X : White

LEFT FRONT
Work as for right front, rev all shapings.

SLEEVES
Using 3,25 mm Ns and A, c/on 36(40;46) sts and work 6 cm in single rib. Change to 4 mm Ns and cont in st st, inc 10(12;14) sts evenly across first row. [46(52;60) sts.] Cont by inc 1 st at each end of every 8th row 9(9;10) times. [64(70;80) sts.]
If you have chosen to work the Fair Isle, begin the motifs when work measures 27(30;34) cm, working 1 motif on each

side of centre 2 sts. When work measures 32(35;39) cm, shape armholes: C/off 3(3;4) sts at the beg of next 2 rows, then 2 sts at the beg of next 2 rows, then 1 st at the beg of next 24(28;32) rows, then 2 sts at the beg of next 2 rows, then 3 sts at the beg of next 4 rows. C/off rem 14 (16;20) sts.

COLLAR
Using 3,25 mm Ns and A, c/on 188(200;212) sts and work in single rib. Work 8 rows straight, then dec 1 st at each end of every 4th row (twice), then 1 st at each end of every alt row (once), then c/off 2 sts at the beg of next 6(10;14) rows, then 3 sts at the beg of next 8 rows, then 4 sts at the beg of next 4 rows, then 5 sts at the beg of next 2 rows. **At the same time**, when work measures 7(8;9) cm work 11 double decs (= slip 1, knit 2 tog, pass slipped stitch over) in the centre of work, spaced 5 sts apart. When the last set of shapings are complete, c/off rem 98(102;106) sts.

FRONT BORDERS
Using 3,25 mm Ns and A, c/on 11 sts and work in single rib.
When work measures 1 cm work 1 buttonhole (3 sts wide), 5 sts in from centre front edge, then work a 2nd buttonhole 5 cm from the first, then work 4 others spaced 6(7;8,5) cm apart. When work measures 31(36;41) cm, c/off.
Work a 2nd border in same way, omitting buttonholes.

TO MAKE UP
Stitch side seams, taking 1 st into the seam.
If you have chosen to work the embroidery, embroider the motifs in Swiss Darning 24(28;33) cm from the lower edge of the back and fronts and 27(30;34) cm from the lower edge of the sleeves. (See the instructions given for Fair Isle.)
Stitch shoulder seams.
Stitch sleeve seams. Sew in sleeves.
Stitch front borders in place.
Sew on the collar.
Stitch pocket linings and borders in place.
Sew on the buttons.

Aran-style cardigan

MATERIALS
Confortable Sport (50 g balls); 9 balls. One pair 5,5 mm and one pair 6 mm knitting needles; 1 cable needle; 7 buttons.

MEASUREMENTS
To fit bust 76 cm.

STITCHES USED
Checks: * P4, K4 *, alternate the sts every 4 rows.
Pattern stitch:
First row: * K1, P1, Cross 2 sts (Cr2; knit into the front of the 2nd stitch, then knit the first stitch, then slip both sts from the left needle).*

2nd row (wrong side): Work sts as set. i.e., K the P sts and P the K sts of previous row. Repeat these 2 rows throughout.
Cables: worked over 4 sts.
First row: K4.
2nd row: P4.
3rd row: Slip 2 sts onto cable needle

BACK
Using 5,5 mm Ns, c/on 61 sts and work in patt st, beg with P2, Cr2, P1. When work measures 6 cm change to 6 mm Ns and cont in checks, inc 1 st on the first row, and beg with P5. When work measures approximately 25 cm after the 9th check is complete, change to 5,5 mm Ns and cont in garter stitch.
When work measures 34 cm beg dec 1 st at each end of every alt row (5 times). Leave the rem 52 sts on spare needle.

LEFT FRONT
Using 5,5 mm Ns, c/on 32 sts and work in patt st, beginning at armhole edge (right hand side of work) with P1. When work measures 6 cm change to 6 mm Ns and cont in check patt, beginning at right hand side of work with K5, and inc 2 sts evenly across first row.
After the 6th check, work pocket opening: Place 16 sts, 9 sts in from armhole edge, on spare N.
Pocket lining (worked separately): Using 6 mm Ns, c/on 18 sts and work 12 cm in st st. Dec 1 st at each end for the seams, then place these sts behind the front in place of the sts left on spare N, then cont in check patt across all sts for front.
After the 9th check, change to 5,5 mm Ns and cont in gst. When work measures 34 cm beg dec 1 st at right hand side of work (armhole edge) on every alt row (5 times). **At the same time**, to shape the curve, leave sts unworked at left hand side of work on every alt row as fols: 12 sts (once), 4 sts (3 times) and 5 sts (once), also working the first 2 sts together on the return rows. [25 sts rem.] Leave work on spare N.

RIGHT FRONT
Work as for left front, rev all shapings.

SLEEVES
Using 5,5 mm Ns, c/on 32 sts and work in patt st, beg with P1. When work measures 6 cm change to 6 mm Ns and cont in check patt, inc 2 sts evenly across first row, and beg with P5. Cont by inc 1 st at each end of every 6th row (7 times), then every 10th row (once) [50 sts]. **At the same time**, when work measures approximately 28 cm (after the 12th row of checks), change to 5,5 mm Ns and cont in gst.
When work measures 36 cm **shape armholes**: dec 1 st at each end of every alt row (5 times). Leave rem 40 sts on spare N.

YOKE
Worked in one piece.
Using 5,5 mm Ns, work across the 25 sts left at the right front, then across the 40 sts of one sleeve, then across the 52 sts on the back, inc 1 st across the back [= 53 sts], then work across the 40 sts of the other sleeve, then across the 25 sts of the left front [183 sts on Ns]. Cont as fols: P2, * 1 cable, P1, K1, P1 *: rep from * to * 25 times in all, then 1 cable and P2.
On the 4th cable twist, reduce each cable to 2 sts and cont in cross sts over the cables [131 sts].
After the 12th row of cross sts, work as fols: P1, K1, * Cr2, 1 double dec (= K the next 2 sts tog, K the next st, then pass the first 2 sts over last st)*. The patt is now set thus: Cr2, K1, etc. . . and 81 sts. After 8 rows, cont in single rib, dec 20 sts evenly across first row. C/off on the 4th row.

TO MAKE UP
Stitch side seams and sleeve seams.

POCKET BORDERS
Using 5,5 mm Ns, rejoin yarn to the sts left at pocket opening and work 3 rows in single rib. C/off on the 4th row.

RIGHT FRONT BORDER
Using 5,5 mm Ns c/on 7 sts and work in single rib, working 7 buttonholes (2 sts wide), 2 sts in from centre front edge; the first is worked 2 cm from the lower edge, the 2nd is worked 4 cm from the first, and the others worked 8,5 cm apart.
When work measures 51 cm c/off.

LEFT FRONT BORDER
Work as for right front border, omitting buttonholes.
Stitch borders in place.
Slip-stitch pocket linings and borders in place.
Sew on the buttons.

and leave at back of work, K the next 2 sts, then K the 2 sts from cable needle. Repeat this cable twist every 4 rows.

TENSION
14½ sts and 20 rows = 10 cm using check pattern and 6 mm Ns.

Ballet outfit

MATERIALS
Pingolaine (50 g balls); **Bolero:** 3(3;4) balls; **Leg Warmers and Headband:** 2 balls (all sizes); 1 pair 3 mm knitting needles.

MEASUREMENTS
To fit chest 61(66;71) cm; length to shoulder 31(32;33) cm; sleeve seam 17(17;18) cm.

TENSION
28 sts and 32 rows = 10 cm over st st, using 3 mm Ns.

Bolero

BACK
C/on 80(84;88) sts and st st 2 rows.

SHAPE SIDES
Inc 1 st at each end of 3rd and every fol 5th row 7(8;9) times. [96(102;108) sts.] Cont straight until work measures 15(16;16) cm from beg, ending with a WS row.

SHAPE ARMHOLES
C/off 3 sts at beg of next 4 rows. Dec 1 st at each end of next and fol 5 alt rows. [72(78;84) sts.] Cont straight until work measures 31(32;33) cm from beg, ending with a WS row.

SHAPE SHOULDERS
C/off 7(8;8) sts at beg of next 4 rows and 7(7;9) sts at beg of fol 2 rows. C/off rem 30(32;34) sts.

LEFT FRONT
C/on 64(68;72) sts and st st 2 rows.

SHAPE SIDES AND FRONT
Inc 1 st at beg (side edge) and dec 1 st at end (front edge) of next row. Cont dec 1 st at front edge every fol 3rd row 21(15;13) times, then every alt row 17(26;31) times. **At the same time** inc 1 st at side edge every fol 5th row 7(8;9) times, then keep this edge straight until work matches back to armhole, ending at side edge.

SHAPE ARMHOLE
C/off 3 sts at beg of this and fol alt row. Dec 1 st at beg of next and fol 5 alt rows. Keep armhole edge straight until work matches back to shoulder. With RS facing work shoulder shapings: c/off 7(8;8) sts at beg of this and next alt row. C/off rem 7(7;9) sts at beg of next alt row.

RIGHT FRONT
Work as for left front, rev shapings.

SLEEVES
C/on 48(48;50) sts and work 3 cm K2, P2 rib, inc 8 sts evenly across last row. [56(56;58) sts.] Cont in st st, inc 1 st at each end of 3rd and every fol 5th row 6(6;7) times. [70(70;74) sts.] Cont straight until work measures 17(17;18) cm from beg, ending with a WS row. V.

SHAPE SLEEVE TOP
C/off 3 sts at beg of next 4 rows. Dec 1 st at each end of next and fol 10(10;8) alt rows. [36(36;44) sts.] C/off 2 sts at beg of next 8(8;12) rows. C/off rem 20 sts.

RIGHT FRONT BAND
Stitch shoulder seams. With RS facing, pick up and K66(68;70) sts along right front edge and 30(32;34) sts across back neck. [96(100;104) sts.] Work 2 cm K2, P2 rib. C/off loosely RW.

LEFT FRONT BAND
With RS facing, pick up and K66 (68;70) sts down left front edge. Complete as for right front band. Stitch ends of bands at shoulder edge.

TIE BELT
C/on 6 sts and work approximately 183 cm K2, P2 rib. C/off RW.

TO MAKE UP
Set in sleeves. Stitch side seams leaving 1,5 cm open at left lower edge. Stitch sleeve seams. Stitch tie belt into position on lower edge, having an equal amount extending from each side, cross over and tie at back.

Legwarmers
C/on 56 sts and work 45 cm K2, P2 rib. V. C/off RW. Stitch seam.

Headband
C/on 100 sts and work 3 cm K2, P2 rib. C/off RW. Stitch seam.
DO NOT IRON.

Hood, mittens and scarves

MATERIALS

Confort DK (50 g balls); **Hood:** 5 balls Red (A); **Mittens and Striped scarf:** 1 ball each Red (A), Yellow (B), Violet (C), Dark Blue (D) and Blue (E). **Scarf:** 4 balls Ecru. One pair 3 mm and 2 pairs 3,75 mm knitting needles.

MEASUREMENTS

To fit 8 year old.

TENSION

26 sts and 30 rows = 10 cm using single rib and 3,75 mm Ns.

Hood

Begin with the top of the hood. Using 3,75 mm Ns, c/on 31 sts and work in single rib. When work measures 11 cm c/on 29 sts at the beg of next 2 rows. [89 sts on Ns.]
When work measures 23 cm shape for the front: c/on 1 st at the beg of next 6 rows, then 2 sts at the beg of next 4 rows, then 3 sts at the beg of next 6 rows, then 5 sts at the beg of next 2 rows. [131 sts on Ns.]
When work measures 40 cm c/off loosely.
Stitch the top of the hood.
Using 3 mm Ns, pick up and K129 sts around the front edge and work 3 cm in single rib. C/off.
Stitch the hood with a fine seam.

Striped scarf

Using 3,75 mm Ns, c/on 51 sts and work in single rib as fols: * 12 rows in A, 12 rows in B, 12 rows in C, 12 rows in E, 12 rows in D *. C/off after the 6th stripe in B.
Make a large pompon in C and one in D. Gather each end of the scarf and stitch a pompon to each end.

Mittens

Using 3 mm Ns and A, c/on 38 sts and work 5 cm in single rib. Change to 3,75 mm Ns and cont in striped st st as fols: * 6 rows in B, 6 rows in C, 6 rows in E, 6 rows in D, 6 rows in A *. On the 3rd row, begin the thumb shaping: inc 1 st at centre of work, then inc 1 st on each side of this centre st on every alt row until there are 11 sts for the thumb. Inc 1 st on the inner edge of the thumb. Divide these 12 sts over the set of 4 Ns and work in rounds. After the stripe in

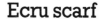

E, cont work in A. On the 13th row of A, work 2 sts tog across the whole of the next row. Break yarn and thread through rem sts. Draw up tightly and fasten off. Rejoin yarn to the other sts and inc 1 st at the base of the thumb on the first row. There are now 39 sts on Ns. On the 2nd row of the 2nd stripe in C, dec 1 st, 2 sts in from each end of row, and dec 1 st on each side of the centre 2 sts, on every alt row (5 times). Work 2 sts tog across the whole of the

next row. Break yarn and thread through rem sts. Draw up tightly and fasten off. Stitch the seam.

Ecru scarf

Using 3,75 mm Ns, c/on 47 sts and work 160 cm in single rib. C/off.
Thread a piece of yarn through each end of scarf and draw up tightly.
Make 2 pompons approximately 8 cm in diameter and stitch one to each end.

School knits

MATERIALS
Challenge 3 (50 g balls); 4(5;5;6;6;7;8) balls; 1 pair each 2,75 mm and 3,75 mm knitting needles; 2,75 mm circular knitting needle.

MEASUREMENTS
To fit chest 66(71;76;81;87;92;97) cm; actual all round measurement 71(75; 81;87;92;97;102) cm; length to back neck 41(46;50;54;59;61;63) cm; sleeve seam 35(37;39;40;41;42;43) cm.

TENSION
26 sts and 28 rows = 10 cm over st st using 3,5 mm Ns.

BACK (for both styles)
Using 2,75 mm Ns, c/on 82(86;92;98; 102;106;110) sts and work 5(5;5;6;6; 6;6) cm K1, P1 rib, inc 10(12;14;16;18; 20;22) sts evenly across last row. [92(98;106;114;120;126;132) sts.]
Change to 3,5 mm Ns and cont in st st until work measures 24(28;31;34;38;39; 40) cm from beg, ending with a WS row. V.

SHAPE RAGLAN
C/off 4(4;4;4;5;5;5) sts at beg of next 2 rows, 3(4;4;4;4;4;4) sts at beg of fol 2 rows and 3(3;3;4;4;4;4) sts at beg of next 2 rows. [72(76;84;90;94;100;106) sts.] ** Dec 1 st at each end of every row 7(7;7;7;5;5;7) times, then 1 st at each end of fol 17(18;20;21;24;25;25) alt rows. C/off rem 24(26;30;34;36; 40;42) sts.

Sweater

FRONT
Work as for back to **

SHAPE NECK
Next row: K2tog, K until there are 35(37;41;44;46;49;52) sts on right N, turn and leave rem 36(38;42;45;47; 50;53) sts on a holder for right front. *** Work raglan shaping as fols: P 1 row, then dec 1 st at beg of next 7(7;7;7;5;5;7) alt rows, then 1 st at beg of fol 17(18;20;21;24;25;25) alt rows. **At the same time** dec 1 st at neck edge on next and every fol 3rd (3rd;2nd;2nd; 2nd;2nd;2nd) row 4(6;5;8;8;11;12) times, then every fol 4th row 6(5;8;7;8; 7;7) times. Fasten off rem 2 sts ***.
Rejoin yarn to neck edge of rem sts and complete to match first side, rev shaping.

Cardigan

LEFT FRONT

Using 2,75 mm Ns, c/on 40(42;46;48; 50;52;54) sts and work 5(5;5;6;6;6; 6) cm K1, P1 rib, inc 6(7;7;9;10;11; 12) sts evenly across last row. [46(49; 53;57;60;63;66) sts.] Change to 3,5 mm Ns and cont in st st until work measures 24(28;31;34;38;39;40) cm from beg, ending with a WS row.

SHAPE RAGLAN AND FRONT

C/off 4(4;4;4;5;5;5) sts at beg of next row 3(4;4;4;4;4;4) sts at beg of fol alt row and 3(3;3;4;4;4;4) sts at beg of next alt row ending with a WS row. [36(38;42;45;47;50;53) sts.] Dec 1 st at beg of next 7(7;7;7;5;5;7) alt rows, then 1 st at beg of fol 17(18;20;21;24;25;25) alt rows. **At the same time,** dec 1 st at neck edge on next and every fol 3rd (3rd;2nd;2nd;2nd;2nd;2nd) row 4(6;5; 8;8;11;12) times, then every fol 4th row 6(5;8;7;8;7;7) times. Fasten off rem 2 sts.

RIGHT FRONT

Work as for left front, rev shapings.

SLEEVES (for both styles)

Using 2,75 mm Ns, c/on 38(42;46;48; 50;52;54) sts and work 5(5;5;6;6;6; 6) cm K1, P1 rib, inc 8 sts evenly across last row. [46(50;54;56;58;60; 62) sts.] Change to 3,5 mm Ns and cont in st st, inc 1 st at each end of next and every fol 4th row 16(17;18;20;22; 22;24) times. [80(86;92;98;104;106; 112) sts.] Cont straight until work measures 35(37;39;40;41;42;43) cm from beg, ending with a WS row. V.

SHAPE RAGLAN

Work as for back raglan. C/off rem 12(14;16;18;20;20;22) sts.

TO MAKE UP

Stitch front and right back raglan seams.

SWEATER NECKBAND

With RS facing, using 2,75 mm Ns, pick up and K21(22;24;25;27;28;29) sts down left front neck edge, 1 st from centre of V (place marker), 21(22;24; 25;27;28;29) sts up right front neck edge and 24(26;30;34;36;40;42) sts across back neck. [67(71;79;85;91; 97;101) sts.] Work 2,5 cm K1, P1 rib, dec 1 st at each side of marked st on every row and, ending with a RS row, K 1 row. Work 2,5 cm K1, P1 rib, inc 1 st at each side of marked st every row.

C/off loosely RW. Stitch rem raglan seam and neckband seam. Fold band in half to WS and slip-st into position.

CARDIGAN BAND

Stitch raglan seams. With RS facing, using circular N, pick up and K58(64; 70;76;84;86;88) sts up right front, 24(26;30;34;36;40;42) sts across back neck and 58(64;70;76;84;86; 88) sts down left front. Work 1 cm K1, P1 rib, ending with a WS row. On next row, work 5 buttonholes evenly spaced between lower edge and start of neck shaping. Cont until band measures 2,5 cm. C/off loosely RW.
Stitch side and sleeve seams.
DO NOT IRON.

Geometric cardigans and sweater

MATERIALS

France + (50 g balls); **Yellow cardigan:** 6(7;8) balls Yellow (A); 1(1;2) balls Black (B); 1 button. **Green cardigan:** 6(7;8) balls Green (A); 1(1;2) balls Black (B); 1 button; 1 pair 4 mm double-pointed knitting needles. **Pink sweater:** 7(7;8) balls Pink (A); 1(1;1) ball Black (B); 1 pair 4 mm double-pointed knitting needles. All garments: 1 pair 3,75 mm knitting needles; 3 stitch holders.

Note: knit with or without motifs, but remember to buy extra colour if Black omitted.

MEASUREMENTS

All garments to fit 81(92;97) cm bust; **Yellow and Green cardigans:** all round measurement 92(96;100,5) cm; length to shoulder 52,5(54,5;56,5) cm; sleeve length 41(42;43) cm. **Pink sweater:** all round measurement 92(96;99) cm; length to shoulder 50(52;54) cm; sleeve length 37 cm.

TENSION

23 sts and 30 rows = 10 cm using st st and 3,75 mm Ns.

Note: all garments – use separate balls of yarn for each colour twisting yarns on wrong side when changing colour.

STITCHES USED

Patt st:

Work from charts for Yellow and Green cardigans.

Yellow top

BACK

Using 3,75 mm Ns and A c/on 106(110;116) sts and beg with a K row work in st st from chart for back. Work 10 rows in A, (beg first pair of blocks winding off 2 small balls of B).

11th row: K2(4;7) sts in A, 22 sts in B, 58 sts in A, 22 sts in B, 2(4;7) sts in A. Cont working from chart 1 until last block has been completed (150 rows

worked from beg). Cont with A and work 8(14;20) rows.

Next row: Cut yarn and sl off 36(38;40) sts onto holder (right back), K next 34(34;36) sts, turn, place rem 36(38;40) sts (left back) onto another holder. Cont on centre 34(34;36) sts and work 9 rows more in st st for back neck border. C/off loosely.

RIGHT FRONT

Using 3,75 mm Ns and A c/on 53(55;58) sts and beg with a K row work in st st fol chart 2; (solid line at centre represents beg of right, or end of left front.) Work 8 rows in A.

9th row (buttonhole): K2, c/off 3, K to end.

Next row: C/on 3 sts over those c/off.

11th row: K2tog for front shaping, K until there are 28 sts on right N, K22 sts in B, 2(4; 7) sts in A. Cont working patt from chart 2 working decs at front edge as shown. When last motif is completed cont with A, working a dec at beg of

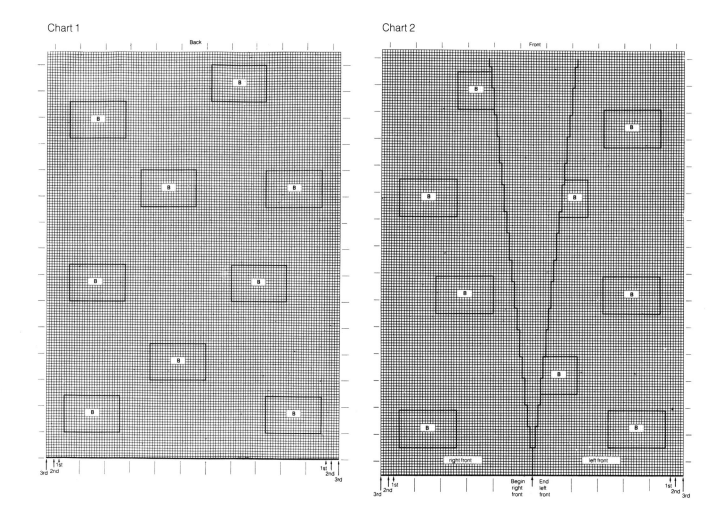

Chart 1

Back

1st
3rd 2nd   1st
                                         2nd 3rd

Chart 2

Front

right front   left front

3rd 2nd 1st   Begin   End   1st
                     right   left   2nd 3rd
                     front   front

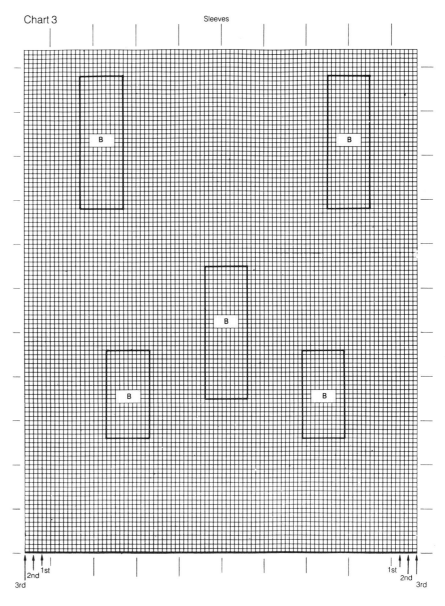

Chart 3   Sleeves

153rd row as shown: **First size:** work 5 rows straight; **2nd size:** work 11 rows straight; **3rd size:** work another dec at beg of 163rd row then 7 rows straight; Cut yarn and leave rem 36(38;40) sts on holder.

LEFT FRONT
Work as for right front omitting buttonhole. For decs work K2tog at end of corresponding rows.

SLEEVES
Using 3,75 mm Ns and A c/on 84(88;92) sts and beg with a K row work in st st fol chart 3 for sleeves. Work 26 rows in A, beg side incs and first pair of blocks.

27th row: Inc in first st, K13(15;17) sts in A, 10 sts in B, 36 sts in A, 10 sts in B, K13(15;17) in A, inc in last st. Cont working from chart inc 1 st at each end of every fol 8th row 10(11;12) times, then every fol 6th row 2(1;0) times.

At the same time after last pair of motifs have been completed on 108th row work 15(18;21) rows in A. C/off 110(114;118) sts.

MAKE UP AND BORDER
Graft shoulder seams. With RS facing using 3,75 mm Ns and A, miss first 10 rows at lower edge of right front and pick up and K113(118;123) sts along rem front edge. Beg with a P row work 10 rows in st st. C/off loosely. Work similar border on left front. Join upper edge of these borders to sides of back neck border working on RS, (when border rolls over seam is hidden). Pin cast-off edge of sleeves to sides of sweater. Stitch into position. Join side and sleeve seams rev seam on 9 rows at lower edge of back and fronts and on 15 rows at lower edge of sleeves. Stitch lower edge of front borders to rows left free on front edges. All borders will roll onto RS. Sew on button.

Green top

BACK
Using 3,75 mm Ns and A, c/on 106(110;116) sts and beg with a K row work in st st from chart 4. Work 18 rows in A.

19th row (beg first motif): K85(87;90) sts in A, 1 st in B, K20(22;25) sts in A. Cont as now set joining on an extra ball of A after 22nd row for this motif and also beg the other motif on 21st row. Cont working from chart until last motif is completed. Work 7(13;19) rows in A ending with a P row.

SHAPE NECK
Next row: K36(38;40), place these sts on holder, c/off next 34(34;36) sts, K to end, place rem 36(38;40) sts on another holder.

RIGHT FRONT
Using 3,75 mm Ns and A c/on 53(55; 58) sts and beg with a K row work 8 rows in st st from chart 4.

9th row (buttonhole): K3, c/off 2, K to

end. On fol row c/on 2 sts over button-hole. Work 8 more rows in A.

19th row: K32 sts in A, join on B and K1 st in B, K20(22;25) sts in A. Cont fol

chart, working dec as shown until 17(17;18) decs have been worked (the last one for 3rd size is not shown on chart). When all motifs have been completed work 8(14;20) rows in A ending with same row as on back. Cut yarn and place sts on holder.

LEFT FRONT
Work as for right front omitting button-hole, rev shapings and working from chart.

SLEEVES
Using 3,75 mm Ns and A, c/on 84(88;92) sts and beg with a K row work in st st working patt from chart 5 for sleeves beg with 10 rows in A.
11th row: K4(6;8) sts in A, join on ball of B and K19 sts in B, join on another ball of A and K39 sts in A, join on another ball of B and K19 sts in B, join on another ball of A and K3(5;7) sts in A. Work 15 more rows from chart.

27th row: inc 1 st at each end of next and every fol 8th row 8(9;9) times, 1 st at each end of every fol 6th row 4(3;4) times. [110(114;120) sts.] After last motif work 2(5;8) rows in A, c/off.

MAKE UP AND BORDER
Graft shoulder seams. With RS facing, using 3 dp Ns and A miss first 10 rows at lower edge of right front, pick up and K119(124;129) sts along rem front edge, 34(34;36) sts across back neck and 119(124;129) sts down front edge of left front leaving last 10 rows free. Using 4th N and beg with a P row work 10 rows in st st then c/off loosely. Join side edges of this border to the rem 10 rows at lower edge making seams on rev side so they are hidden when border rolls over. Pin c/off edge of sleeves to sides of cardigan. Stitch into position. Stitch side and sleeve seams rev seam on 10th row at lower edge of each. Sew on button.

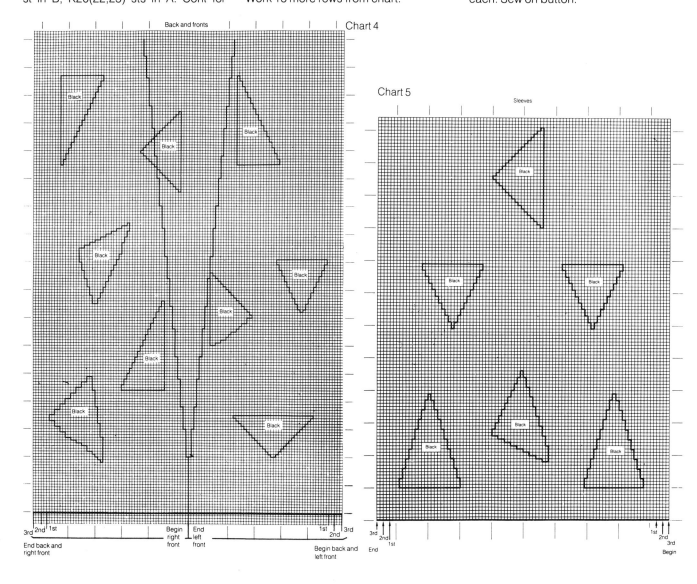

Pink top

FRONT
Using 3,75 mm Ns and A, c/on 106(110;114) sts and work in st st beg with a K row. Work 30(34;38) rows then beg panels:
First row: K6 sts in A, join on B, K72 sts in B, join on another ball of A, K28(32;36) sts in A.
2nd row: P28(32;36) sts in A, 72 sts in B, 6 sts in A. Work 4 more rows as now set, work 12 rows A.
19th row: K26(30;34) sts in A, 72 sts in B, 8 sts in A.
20th row: P8 sts in A, 72 sts in B, 26(30;34) sts in A. Work 4 more rows as now set, work 26 rows in A.
51st row: K42 sts in A, 64(68;72) sts in B.
52nd row: P64(68;72) sts in B, 42 sts in A. Work 4 more rows as now set, work 26 rows in A.
83rd row: K76 sts in B, 30(34;38) sts in A.
84th row: P30(34;38) sts in A, 76 sts in B. Work 4 rows as now set, cont with A only. Work 4(6;8) rows.

SHAPE NECK
First row: K44(45;47) sts for left front; sl next 18(20;20) sts onto dp N and rem 44(45;47) sts of right front onto holder. Cont on left front sts.

2nd and alt rows: P to end.
3rd row: K38(39;41), turn and place rem 6 sts onto dp N. Cont leaving sts unworked at end of each RS row placing them onto dp N as fols: 5 sts (once), 4 sts (once), 3 sts (twice), 2 sts (twice) and 1 st (6 times). Turn, P to end. C/off rem 13(14;16) sts for shoulder.
With RS facing rejoin A to sts of right front, K to end.
2nd row: P38(39;41) turn, place 6 sts onto dp N. Cont in this way and complete as for left front.

BACK
Work as for front for the first 30(34;38) rows. Work panels which are in rev positions to those of front.
First row: K28(32;36) sts in A, 72 sts in B, 6 sts in A. Work 5 more rows as now set, then work 12 rows in A.
19th row: K8 sts in A, 72 sts in B, 26(30;34) sts in A. Work 5 more rows as now set, then work 26 rows in A.
51st row: K64(68;72) sts in B, 42 sts in A. Work 5 more rows as set, then work 26 rows in A.
83rd row: K30(34;38) sts in A, 76 sts in B. Work 5 more rows as set, then cont with A. Work 14(16;18) rows.

SHAPE NECK
First row: K40(41;43) sts for right back; sl next 26(28;28) sts onto dp N and rem 40(41;43) sts of left back on holder. Cont on right back sts.
2nd and alt rows: P to end.
3rd row: K34(35;37), turn, place rem 6 sts onto dp N. Cont leaving sts unworked on RS rows as fols: 4 sts (4 times), 2 sts (twice) and 1 st (once). Turn, P to end. C/off rem 13(14;16) sts.
With RS facing rejoin A to sts of left back, K to end.
2nd row: P34(35;37), turn and place 6 sts onto dp N. Complete as for right back.

RIGHT SLEEVE
Using 3,75 mm Ns and A, c/on 84(88;92) sts and work in st st beg with a K row; inc 1 st at each end of every fol

10th row (5 times), and every fol 8th row (6 times). **At the same time,** work 12 rows in A, 6 rows in B, 12 rows in A.
31st row: K34(36;38) sts in B, 22 sts in A, join on 2nd ball of B, K34(36;38) sts in B. Cont as now set for 5 more rows still working incs, then cont with A for 46 rows.
83rd row: K24(26;28) sts in A, 54 sts in B, 24(26;28) sts in A. ** Cont as now set for 5 more rows working rem inc on correct rows. **At the same time,** work 10 rows in A, 6 rows in B, 8 rows in A. C/off 106(110;114) sts.

LEFT SLEEVE
Using 3,75 mm Ns and A, c/on 84(88;92) sts and work in st st with incs as right sleeve but in fol order of colours: 16 rows in A, 6 rows in B, 16 rows in A.
39th row: K21(23;25) sts in A, 48 sts in B, 21(23;25) sts in A. Cont as set inc at each end of next row, then work 4 rows straight. Cont working incs on correct rows and work 38 rows in A.
83rd row: K40(42;44) sts in B, 22 sts in A, 40(42;44) sts in B. Complete as for right sleeve from ** to end.

NECK BORDER AND YOKE
With RS facing and using A, K the 80(82;82) sts from dp N at front neck. Beg with a P row work 6 rows in st st. C/off loosely. Work similar border on back. Fold front border down onto RS, and with RS facing and using A pick up and K80(82;82) sts into back of sts in first row of neck border. Beg with a P row work 12 cm in st st. C/off loosely. Work back yoke in same way, picking up 72(74;74) sts.

TO MAKE UP
Stitch shoulder seams, join seams of yoke but rev seam on last 9 rows at top. Stitch seams of neck border on rev side. Pin cast-off edge of sleeves to sides of sweater. Stitch into position. Stitch side and sleeve seams rev seam on 9 rows at lower edge of each seam.

Man's slipover

MATERIALS
4 Pingouin (50 g balls); 7(8;9) balls.
Two pairs 3 mm and 1 pair 3,75 mm
knitting needles; 1 cable needle.

MEASUREMENTS
To fit chest 92-97 (102-107;112-
117) cm.

STITCHES USED
Cable over 6 sts worked thus: slip next
3 sts on cable needle, leave at front,
K3, then K3 from cable needle. For the
cable and rib patt see text.

TENSION
28 sts and 37 rows = 10 cm over patt
using 3,75 mm Ns.

BACK
With 3 mm Ns c/on 145(153;159) sts
and work in single rib for 7 cm. Change
to 3,75 mm Ns and patt.
First row (right side): For **first size** P3
(for **2nd size** K2, P5; for **3rd size** P2, K3,
P5), then for all sizes * K6 for a cable,
P5, K3, P5; rep from * 6 times more. K6
for a cable, then for **first size** P3 (for **2nd
size** P5, K2; for **3rd size** P5, K3, P2).
2nd row: Work sts as set – P the sts
which were worked K on previous row
and K the P sts.
3rd row: As first but work the cable over
each group of 6 sts.
4th row to 20th row: Rep 2nd row once
then first and 2nd rows 8 times. These

20 rows form patt. Cont in patt until
work measures 38(40;42) cm from beg
ending with a WS row.

ARMHOLE SHAPING
C/off 6(7;8) sts at beg of next 2 rows, 4
sts at beg of next 2 rows, 3 sts at beg of
next 2 rows, 2 sts at beg of next 4 rows
and 1 st at beg of next 4 rows. Cont on
rem 107(113;117) sts until work measures 63(65;68) cm from beg ending
with a WS row.

SHOULDER AND NECK SHAPING
C/off 10(11;11) sts at beg of next 2
rows.
3rd row: C/off 10(11;11), patt until there
are 16(16;17) sts on right N, leave these
for right back. C/off next 35(37;39) sts,
patt to end. Cont on 26(27;28) sts now
rem at end of N for left back. C/off
10(11;11) sts at beg of next row and 5
sts at neck edge on fol row. C/off rem
11(11;12) sts. Rejoin yarn to neck edge
of right back sts, c/off 5, patt to end.
C/off rem 11(11;12) sts.

FRONT
Work as for back until you have worked
8(4;4) rows of armhole shaping, then
divide for neck. Still shaping armholes
as for back, on fol row c/off centre st
and complete each side separately
working first on sts of right front. Dec 1
st at neck edge on next 5(6;7) alt rows
then at same edge on every fol 4th row
17 times. Meanwhile when armhole

shaping is completed keep this edge
straight until work matches back to
shoulder, ending at side.

SHOULDER SHAPING
C/off 10(11;11) sts at beg of next row
and next alt row. Work 1 row then c/off
rem 11(11;12) sts.
Rejoin yarn to neck edge of left front sts
and complete as for right front rev all
shapings.

NECK BORDER
Join shoulder seams matching patt.
With RS of work facing and using 3 mm
Ns, pick up and K68(71;74) sts up right
front neck edge, 42(44;46) sts across
back neck and 68(71;74) sts down left
front neck. You will need to use 2 pairs
of Ns picking up sts onto 3 Ns and
working with the 4th. Work 1 row in
single rib then keeping rib correct dec
1 st at both ends of next 6 rows. C/off
RW. Join shaped ends forming a point
at centre front.

ARMHOLE BORDERS
With RS of work facing and using 3 mm
Ns, pick up and K150(150;156) sts all
round one armhole edge. Work in
single rib for 7 rows. C/off RW. Work
other armhole border in same way. Join
side seams and the ends of armhole
borders.

Classic twosome

Lady's Fair Isle cardigan

MATERIALS
Poudreuse (50 g balls); 4(5;6) balls Blue (A); 3(4;5) balls White (B). One pair each 3,75 mm and 4,5 mm knitting needles; 7 buttons.

MEASUREMENTS
To fit bust 81-87 (92-97; 102-107) cm.

STITCHES USED
Fair Isle patt Work from chart. As different parts of the patt have different numbers of sts for the patt repeat, knitters may prefer to draw their own chart. Use a piece of squared paper of the width required for the number of sts, mark the centre as indicated on our chart and extend the pattern in both directions until it reaches the sides. From this you can see where to begin your rows. When working right front begin at the

point indicated on our chart and mark on your chart the point at which you will end. The left front will be the reverse of this. On the sleeve mark on your chart the centre st and count to each side for the number of sts on the sleeve. Note

that the pattern on the sleeve begins on the 31st row so that the pattern will match at the armholes.

TENSION
23 sts and 23 rows = 10 cm over patt using 4,5 mm Ns.

BACK
With 3,75 mm Ns and A, c/on 115(121;125) sts and work in single rib for 7 cm. Change to 4,5 mm Ns and working in st st beg with a K row work patt from chart. Cont until work measures 37(38;39) cm from beg, ending with a P row.

ARMHOLE SHAPING
C/off 4 sts at beg of next 2 rows, 3 sts at beg of next 2 rows, 2 sts at beg of next 2 rows and 1 st at beg of next 10(12;12) rows. Cont on rem 87(91;95) sts until work measures 56(58;60) cm from beg, ending with a P row.

SHOULDER AND NECK SHAPING

C/off 8(9;10) sts at beg of next 2 rows.
3rd row: C/off 8(9;10), patt until there are 17 sts on right N, leave these for right back, c/off next 21 sts, patt to end. Cont on 25(26;27) sts now rem at end of N for left back. C/off 8(9;10) sts at beg of next row and 8 sts at neck edge on fol row. C/off rem 9 sts. Rejoin yarns to neck edge of right back sts. C/off 8, patt to end. C/off rem 9 sts.

RIGHT FRONT

With 3,75 mm Ns and A, c/on 60(63;65) sts and work in single rib for 7 cm. Change to 4,5 mm Ns and working in st st work patt from chart. Cont until you have worked 1 more row than on back to armhole thus ending at side.

ARMHOLE SHAPING

C/off 4 sts at beg of next row, 3 sts at same edge on next alt row, 2 sts on next alt row and 1 st on next 7(8;8) alt rows. Cont on rem 44(46;48) sts until you have worked 14 rows fewer than on back to beg of shoulder, thus ending at front edge.

NECK AND SHOULDER SHAPING

C/off 8 sts at beg of next row, 3 sts at same edge on next alt row, 2 sts on next 2 alt rows and 1 st on next 4 alt rows. Now c/off for shoulder, 8(9;10) sts at beg of next row and next alt row. Work 1 row then c/off rem 9 sts.

LEFT FRONT

Work as for right front rev patt and all shapings.

SLEEVES

With 3,75 mm Ns and A c/on 48(50;54) sts and work in single rib for 7 cm then change to 4,5 mm Ns and K 1 row working 22(24;24) incs evenly spaced. [70(74;78) sts.] P 1 row on these sts then work in patt beg at row indicated and inc 1 st at both ends of every fol 8th row 6(7;8) times, then every fol 6th row 3(2;1) times working sts into patt. Cont on 88(92;96) sts until work measures approx 42(43;44) cm from beg, ending at same position in patt as before armhole on back.

TOP SHAPING

C/off 4 sts at beg of next 2 rows, 3 sts at beg of next 2 rows, 2 sts at beg of next 2 rows, 1 st at beg of next 26(28;30) rows, 3 sts at beg of next 6 rows and 4 sts at beg of next 2 rows. C/off rem 18(20;22) sts.

FRONT BORDERS

With 3,75 mm Ns and A c/on 11 sts.
First row (right side): K2, * P1, K1; rep from * to last st, K1.
2nd row: K1, * P1, K1; rep from * to end. Rep these 2 rows until work measures 3(2,5;3,5) cm from beg, ending with a WS row, then make buttonhole.
Next row: Rib 4, c/off 3, rib to end. On fol row c/on 3 sts over buttonhole. Make 5 more buttonholes each 8(8,5;8,5) cm above cast-off edge of previous one then cont until border matches front edge of right front ending with a WS row. Leave sts on a holder. Work similar border for left front omitting buttonholes.

NECKBAND

Join shoulder seams. Sew on front borders. With RS facing and using 3,75 mm Ns and A, rib sts of right front border, pick up and K29 sts along right front neck, 41 sts across back neck and 29 sts along left front neck edge then rib sts of left front border. Cont in rib across all sts for 1(3;1) rows, make another buttonhole at right front edge on next 2 rows then work 5(3;5) rows. C/off RW.

TO MAKE UP

Sew in sleeves then join side and sleeve seams. Sew on buttons.

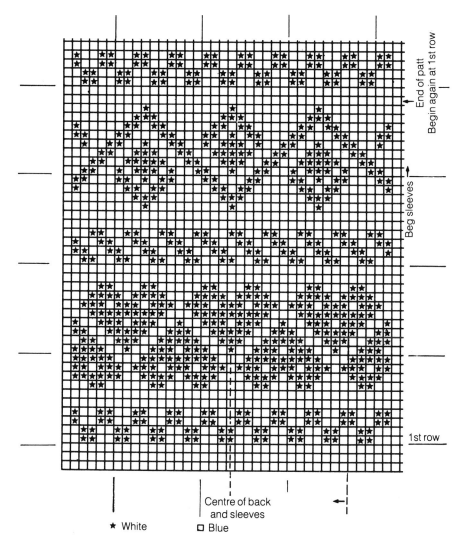

End of patt
Begin again at 1st row

Beg sleeves

1st row

Centre of back
and sleeves

★ White   □ Blue

Man's fisherman's rib sweater

MATERIALS
France + (50 g balls); 7(8;9;10;11) balls Pale Blue (A); 3 balls White (B); 2 balls Dark Blue (C). One pair each 3 mm and 3,75 mm knitting needles.

MEASUREMENTS
To fit chest 87(92;97;102;107) cm.

STITCHES USED
Single-sided Fishermans rib worked as fols:
First row (right side): K all sts.
2nd row: K1, P1, * K next st but in the row below inserting N through work and allowing st above to drop off needle, P1; rep from * to last st, K1. These 2 rows form patt.

TENSION
25 sts and 44 rows = 10 cm over patt using 3,75 mm Ns.

BACK
With 3 mm Ns and A c/on 125(131;135; 139;145) sts and work in single rib beg and ending RS rows with P1 and WS rows with K1. Cont until work measures 8 cm ending with a WS row. Change to 3,75 mm Ns and patt. Cont until work measures 31(33;35;37;39) cm from beg, ending with a 2nd row. Now work the stripes, always changing colour after a 2nd patt row. ** Work 3 cm in B then 9 cm in C, then complete work in B. ** **At the same time** cont without shaping until work measures 34(36; 38;40;42) cm from beg, ending with a 2nd patt row.

RAGLAN SHAPING
*** Place a marker loop of contrasting yarn at each end of last row to indicate beg of armhole. Work 2 rows straight.
3rd row: K3, K3tog, K to last 6 sts, sl 1, K2tog, pass slipped st over, K3. Work 1 row in patt. Rep last 4 rows 20(21;22;23;24) times more. Work a further 4 rows in patt. *** C/off rem 41(43;43;43;45) sts.

FRONT
Work as given for back but after working the last dec row shape neck. On fol row (wrong side) patt 9 and leave these sts of right front, c/off next 23(25; 25;25;27) sts, patt to end. Cont on last set of 9 sts casting off at neck edge on alt rows 3 sts (3 times). Rejoin yarn to 9 sts of right front and complete in same way rev shapings.

SLEEVES
With 3 mm Ns and A, c/on 57(63;67;71; 77) sts and work in single rib as on back for same number of rows. Change to 3,75 mm Ns and work in patt but inc 1 st at both ends of every fol 10th row 2(4;6;8;10) times, then every fol 8th row 4 times, then every fol 6th row 12(10;8;6;4) times working sts into patt. [93(99;103;107;113) sts.] **At the same time,** when work measures 35(37;39;41;43) cm from beg, ending with a 2nd row work the stripes as on back from ** to **. Meanwhile after shapings are completed cont until work measures 38(40;42;44;46) cm from beg, ending with a 2nd patt row. Work raglan shaping as on back from *** to ***. C/off rem 9(11;11;11;13) sts.

MAKE UP AND NECKBAND
Join front raglan seams and right back seam. With RS of work facing and using 3 mm Ns and B, pick up and K100(108;108;108;116) sts all round neck edge. Work in single rib for 4 cm. C/off loosely RW.
Join left back raglan seam and ends of neckband. Fold band in half to WS and slip-st cast-off edge to back of picked-up sts. Join side and sleeve seams.

Bright stripes

MATERIALS
Sweet hair (50 g balls); 4(4;5) balls White (A); 2 balls Green (B); 1 ball Pink (C); 2(3;3) balls Purple (D); 1 pair each 3 mm and 6 mm knitting needles.

MEASUREMENTS
To fit bust 71-76(82-87; 92-97) cm; actual all round measurement 94(100; 105) cm; length to shoulder 56 cm; sleeve length 37 cm.

TENSION
Work one narrow stripe and one wide stripe as given below.
23 sts = 10 cm over st st using 3 mm Ns, one narrow stripe and 1 wide stripe = 8 cm.

STRIPE SEQUENCE
Work 10 rows st st in each colour, changing Ns and colours as fols: * 6 mm Ns and B, 3 mm Ns and A, 6 mm Ns and C, 3 mm Ns and A, 6 mm Ns and D **, 3 mm Ns and A ***.

BACK AND FRONT (alike)
Using 3 mm Ns and A, c/on 96(102; 106) sts and work 5 cm K2, P2 rib, inc 16(18;20) sts evenly across last row. [112(120;126) sts.] Work as given above from * to ***, then from * to **.
Change to 3 mm Ns and A and work 3 cm K2, P2 rib. C/off loosely RW.

SLEEVES (for all sizes)
Using 3 mm Ns and A, c/on 50 sts and work 8 cm K2, P2 rib, ending with a RS row.
Inc row: Rib 3, inc into each of next 44 sts, rib 3. [94 sts.] Work stripe sequence as given above from * to **. Using 6 mm Ns and A, work 8 cm K2, P2 rib. C/off loosely RW.

TO MAKE UP
Stitch shoulder seams, leaving 30 cm for neck opening. Place a marker 25 cm down from each side of shoulders. Stitch cast-off edge of sleeve between markers.
Stitch side and sleeve seams.
DO NOT IRON.

Striped tops for two

MATERIALS

Challenge 3 (50 g balls); **Lady's:** 2 balls Red (A); 3 balls Blue (B) and 3 balls White (C); **Man's:** 6(7;7;8;8) balls Ecru (A); 2 balls Red (B); 1 ball Blue (C) and 1 ball Yellow (D); 1 pair each 3 mm and 3,75 mm knitting needles; 3 buttons for Man's top; stitch holder.

MEASUREMENTS

Lady's: to fit bust 81-87(92-97) cm loosely; actual all round measurement 100(104) cm; length to shoulder 60 (61) cm; sleeve seam 45 cm.
Man's: to fit chest 87(92;97;102; 107) cm; actual all round measurement 96(100;108;112;116) cm; length to shoulder 61(64;67;70;72) cm; sleeve seam 42(44;46;48;50) cm.

TENSION

24 sts and 32 rows = 10 cm over striped st st, using 3,75 mm Ns.

Lady's top

BACK

Using 3 mm Ns and A, c/on 115(120) sts and work 7 cm K1, P1 rib, inc 10 sts evenly across last row. [125(130) sts.] Change to 3,75 mm Ns and cont in striped st st working 6 rows B, 6 rows C throughout *, until work measures 41 cm from beg, ending with a WS row.

SHAPE ARMHOLES

C/off 4(5) sts at beg of next 2 rows, 3 sts at beg of fol 2 rows and 2 sts at beg of next 4 rows. Dec 1 st at each end of next 4 alt rows. [95(98) sts.] Cont straight until work measures 60(61) cm from beg, ending with a WS row. V.

SHAPE SHOULDERS AND NECK

Next row: C/off 7 sts, K until there are 19(20) sts on right N, leave these sts for

right back, c/off next 43(44) sts, K to end. Cont on 26(27) sts rem at end of N for left back. C/off 7 sts at beg of next and fol alt row and 6 sts at neck edge on fol row. Work 1 row. C/off rem 6(7) sts. Rejoin yarn to neck edge of rem sts and complete to match first side.

FRONT

Work as for back to *, cont until work measures 31(32)cm from beg, ending with a WS row. V.

SHAPE NECK

Next row: K62(65) sts, turn and leave rem sts on a holder for right front. Dec 1 st at neck edge every fol 3rd row 22(24) times, then dec 1 st at same edge of every fol 4th row 5(4) times. **At the same time**, when work matches back to armhole, shape armhole: c/off 4(5) sts at beg of next row, then 3 sts at beg of next alt row, then 2 sts at beg of next 2 alt rows. Dec 1 st at beg of next 4 alt rows. Cont straight until work matches back to shoulder, ending with a WS row.

SHAPE SHOULDER

With RS facing, c/off 7 sts at beg of next and fol alt row and rem 6(7) sts on next alt row. Rejoin yarn to neck edge of rem sts (for **first size** c/off 1 st). K to end. Complete to match first side rev shapings.

LEFT SLEEVE

Using 3 mm Ns and A, c/on 50 sts and work 7 cm K1, P1 rib, inc 20(24) sts evenly across last row. [70(74) sts.] Change to 3,75 mm Ns and cont in striped st st, inc 1 st at each end of every 14th row 8 times. [86(90) sts.] **At the same time**, after the 8th stripe in B, work 30 rows in A.

SHAPE SLEEVE TOP

Cont in striped st st. C/off 4 sts at beg of next 2 rows, 3 sts at beg of fol 2 rows, 2 sts at beg of next 4(6) rows. Dec 1 st at each end of next 13 alt rows. C/off 3 sts at beg of next 4 rows and 4 sts at beg of fol 2 rows. C/off rem 18 sts.

RIGHT SLEEVE

Work as for left sleeve in plain striped st st, omitting the wide stripe in A.

RIGHT HALF COLLAR

Using 3 mm Ns and A, c/on 155 sts and work 2 rows K1, P1 rib. Cont in rib, c/off 5 sts at beg of next and fol 19 alt rows. Work 1 row, c/off rem 55 sts.

LEFT HALF COLLAR
Work as for right half, rev shapings.

TO MAKE UP
Stitch shoulder seams. Set in sleeves and stitch into position. Stitch side and sleeve seams matching stripes. Stitch back collar seam. Stitch straight edge of front collar seam for 9 cm, forming a point. Stitch collar into position.

Man's top

BACK
Using 3 mm Ns and A, c/on 110(116; 120;124;128) sts and work 8 cm K1, P1 rib, inc 6(6;10;10;10) sts evenly across last row. [116(122;130;134;138) sts.] Change to 3,75 mm Ns and cont in striped st st as follows:
* 4 rows B, 24 rows A, 4 rows D, 24 rows A, 4 rows C, 24 rows A *; rep from * to * throughout. Cont straight until work measures 42(44;46;48;50) cm from beg, ending with a WS row. V.

SHAPE ARMHOLES
C/off 4(4;5;6;6) sts at beg of next 2 rows, 3(4;4;4;4) sts at beg of fol 2 rows and 2(3;2;2;3) sts at beg of next 2 rows. Dec 1 st at each end of next and fol 2(1;3;3;3) alt rows. [92(96;100;102; 104) sts.] ** Cont straight until work measures 61(64;67;70;72) cm from beg, ending with a WS row.

SHAPE SHOULDERS
C/off 7 sts at beg of next 2 rows.
Next row: C/off 7 sts, K until there are 23(24;25;26;26) sts on right N, leave these sts for right back, c/off next 18(20;22;22;24) sts, K to end. Cont on 30(31;32;33;33) sts rem at end of N for left back. C/off 7 sts at beg of next row and 10 sts at neck edge at beg of fol row. C/off 7(7;7;8;8) sts at beg of next row and 6(7;8;8;8) sts at beg of fol alt row. Rejoin yarn to neck edge of rem sts and complete to match first side.

FRONT
Work as for back to **. Cont straight until work measures 55(58;60;63;64) cm ending with a WS row.

SHAPE NECK
Next row: K until there are 38(40;42; 43;43) sts on right N, leave these sts on a holder for left front, c/off next 16(16;16;16;18) sts, K to end. Cont on 38(40;42;43;43) sts rem on N for right front. P 1 row. C/off at neck edge on next and fol alt rows 4 sts (once), 3 sts (once) and 2 sts (once). Dec 1 st at same edge on next and fol 1(2;3;3;3) alt rows. Cont straight until work matches back to shoulder, ending at side edge.

SHAPE SHOULDER
C/off 7 sts at beg of next and fol alt row, 7(7;7;8;8) sts at beg of next alt row. Work 1 row. C/off rem 6(7;8;8;8) sts. Rejoin yarn to neck edge of rem sts and complete to match first side, rev shapings.

SLEEVES
Using 3 mm Ns and A, c/on 52(54;56; 56;58) sts and work 8 cm K1, P1 rib, inc 14(14;14;16;16) sts evenly across last row. [66(68;70;72;74) sts.] Change to 3,75 mm Ns and cont in striped st st, inc 1 st at each end of every 8th(8th;10th;10th;10th) row 11 times. [88(90;92;94;96) sts.] Cont straight until work measures 42(44;46;48;50) cm from beg, ending with a WS row. V.

SHAPE SLEEVE TOP
C/off 4(4;5;4;4) sts at beg of next 2 rows.*** C/off 2 sts at beg of next 2 rows, c/off 1 st at beg of fol 2 rows; rep from *** 9(9;9;10;10) times in all. C/off 3 sts at beg of next 4 rows. C/off rem 14(16;16;14;16) sts

NECKBAND
Stitch right shoulder seam. With RS facing, using 3 mm Ns and A, pick up and K 58(62;66;66;70) sts around front neck and 36(38;40;40;42) sts across back neck. [94(100;106;106;112) sts.] Work 2 cm K1, P1 rib. C/off loosely RW.

BUTTONHOLE BAND
With RS facing using 3 mm Ns and A, pick up and K36(36;38;40;40) sts across left front shoulder, including neckband. Work 1,5 cm K1, P1 rib.
Next row (buttonholes): Rib 5 sts, [c/off 2 sts, rib 10(10;11;12;12) sts] twice, c/off 2 sts, rib to end. On next row, c/on 2 sts over c/off sts to complete buttonholes. When rib measures 3 cm, c/off loosely RW.

BUTTON BAND
Work as for Buttonhole Band, picking up across back shoulder seam and neckband, omitting buttonholes.

TO MAKE UP
Lap front band over back band and stitch along side edges. Set in sleeves and stitch into position. Stitch side and sleeve seams matching stripes. Sew on buttons.

V-neck sweater dress

MATERIALS
Confort DK (50 g balls); 10(11;12) balls; 1 pair each 3 mm and 3,75 mm knitting needles.

MEASUREMENTS
To fit chest 71(76; 81-86) cm; actual all round measurement 81(92;97) cm; length to shoulder 58(63;67) cm; sleeve seam 36(38; 40) cm.

TENSION
22 sts and 40 rows = 10 cm over patt using 3,75 mm Ns.

STITCHES USED
Beaded rib: Work as for K1, P1 rib, inserting needle into centre of K stitch, one row below on wrong side rows.

BACK
Using 3 mm Ns, c/on 89(101;107) sts and work 6 cm K1, P1 rib. Change to 3,75 mm Ns and cont in beaded rib.* When work measures 50(54;56) cm from beg, shape armholes: c/off 5 sts at the beg of next 2 rows, 4 sts at beg of next 2 rows, 2(3;3) sts at beg of next 2 rows, then 1 st at the beg of next 2 rows. [65(75;81) sts.]
When work measures 58(63;67) cm from beg, shape shoulders: c/off 2 sts at the beg of next 18(20;22) rows. C/off rem 29(35;37) sts.

FRONT
Begin work as given for back to *. Cont straight until work measures 49(53; 55) cm from beg.

SHAPE NECK
C/off centre 1 st, then cont each side separately, dec 1 st at neck edge on every alt row 16(19;20) times. At the same time, when work measures 50(54;56) cm from beg, shape armholes: c/off at beg of alt rows 5 sts (once), 4 sts (once), 2(3;3) sts (once), 1 st (once). When work measures 58(63; 67) cm from beg, shape shoulder: c/off at armhole edge on every alt row as fols: 2 sts 8(9;10) times.

RIGHT SLEEVE
Using 3 mm Ns, c/on 45(49;51) sts and work 6(7;7) cm K1, P1 rib. Change to 3,75 mm Ns and cont in beaded rib, inc 1 st at each end of every 8th row 12(13;15) times. [69(75;81) sts.] Cont straight until work measures 36(38;40)

cm from beg, then shape armholes: c/off 2 sts at the beg of next 12 rows, then dec 1 st at each end of every alt row 13(15;17) times. [19(21;23) sts.] Work 7(8;9) cm straight, then c/off at right hand side of work on every alt row as fols: 6(7;7) sts (once), 6(7;8) sts (once), 7(7;8) sts (once).

LEFT SLEEVE
Work as for right sleeve, rev shapings.

TO MAKE UP
Stitch shoulder extensions in place. Sew in sleeves, stitch side and sleeve seams.

NECK BORDER
Using 3 mm Ns, c/on 59(69;75) sts and work in single rib, beg and ending with P2, and dec 1 st at each end of every row. When work measures 3 cm, c/off. Stitch neck border seam into a point. Sew border to neck.

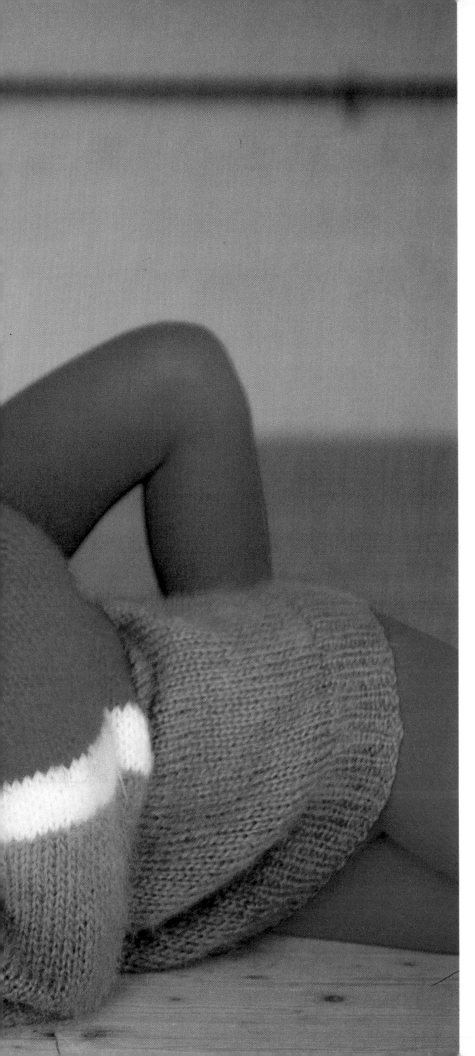

Bright roll-neck sweaters

MATERIALS
Mohair extra (50 g balls); **Set-in-sleeve sweater:** 6(7) balls Green (A); 4 balls per size Blue (B); 1 ball per size Red (C); **Raglan sleeve sweater:** 6(7) Green (A); 2 balls each per size White (B), Red (C), Orange (D) and Pink (E); 1 pair each 5,5 mm and 8 mm knitting needles.

MEASUREMENTS
To fit bust 87-92(97-102) cm; actual all round measurement 104(108) cm; **Set-in-sleeve sweater:** length to shoulder 58(60) cm; sleeve seam 44(45) cm; **Raglan-sleeve sweater:** length to back neck 58(60) cm; sleeve seam 42(43) cm.

TENSION
12 sts and 16 rows = 10 cm over st st using 8 mm Ns.

Set-in-sleeve sweater with separate collar

BACK
Using 5,5 mm Ns and A, c/on 58(61) sts and work 8 cm K1, P1 rib. Change to 8 mm Ns and cont in st st, inc 4 sts evenly across first row. [62(65) sts.] When work measures 39(40) cm from beg, ending with a WS row, work 4 rows in C, then complete work in B. **At the same time, shape armholes:** c/off 3 sts at the beg of next 2 rows, 2 sts at beg of fol 2 rows, then 1 st at beg of next 6(8) rows. [46(47) sts.]
Work until measures 58(60) cm from beg, ending with a WS row.

SHAPE SHOULDERS AND NECK

C/off 4 sts at the beg of next 2 rows.
Next row: C/off 4 sts, K until there are 9 sts on right N, leave these for right back, c/off next 12(13) sts, K to end. Cont on 13 sts rem at end of N for left back. C/off 4 sts at beg of next row. C/off 6 sts at beg of fol row (neck edge). C/off rem 3 sts. Complete other side to match, rev all shapings.

FRONT

Work as given for back until work measures 55(57) cm from beg, ending with a WS row.

SHAPE NECK

Next row: K until there are 18 sts on right N and leave these for left front, c/off next 10(11) sts, K to end. Cont on 18 sts rem on N and P 1 row. C/off at beg of next and fol alt rows, 4 sts (once), 2 sts (once) and 1 st (once). When work measures 58(60) cm from beg, ending at side edge, **shape shoulder:** c/off 4 sts at beg of next row, then 4 sts at beg of next alt row. C/off rem 3 sts. Complete 2nd side to match, rev all shapings.

SLEEVES

Using 5,5 mm Ns and A, c/on 23(26) sts and work 8 cm K1, P1 rib. Change to 8 mm Ns and cont in st st, inc 12 sts evenly across first row. [35(38) sts.] Cont by inc 1 st at each end of every 10th row (4 times). [43(46) sts.] When work measures 44(45) cm from beg, ending with a WS row, work 4 rows in C, then complete work in B. **At the same time, shape armholes:** c/off 3 sts at beg of next 2 rows, 2 sts at beg of fol 2 rows, 1 st at beg of next 8(10) rows, 2 sts at beg of fol 4 rows, then 3 sts at beg of next 2 rows. C/off remaining 11(12) sts.

TO MAKE UP

Stitch right shoulder seam. Using 5,5 mm Ns and B, pick up and K31(32)

sts around front neck, then 27(28) sts across back neck. [58(60) sts.] Work 2,5 cm K1, P1 rib. C/off RW. Stitch left shoulder and neckband seam. Set in sleeves. Stitch side and sleeve seams.

SEPARATE ROLL COLLAR

Using 8 mm Ns and B, c/on 60(62) sts and work 22 cm in st st. C/off. Stitch seam.

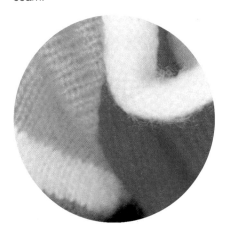

Raglan-sleeve sweater

BACK

Using 5,5 mm Ns and A, c/on 58(61) sts and work 8 cm K1, P1 rib. Change to 8 mm Ns and cont in st st, inc 4 sts evenly across first row. [62(65) sts.] When work measures 32(33) cm from beg ending with a WS row, work 6 rows in B, then complete work in C. **At the same time,** when work measures 34(35) cm from beg, ending with a WS row*, **shape raglan:** c/off 3 sts at beg of next 2 rows, 2 sts at beg of next 2 rows, dec 1 st at each end of fol 17(18) alt rows. C/off rem 18(19) sts.

FRONT

As for back until 28(29) sts rem, ending with a WS row.

SHAPE NECK

Cont to dec 1 st at raglan edge on alt rows, **at the same time,** c/off centre 8(9) sts and complete each side at the same time, using separate balls of yarn. C/off at each neck edge on alt row, 4 sts (once) and 2 sts (once). C/off rem 1 st.
Note: front is 4 rows shorter than back.

RIGHT SLEEVE

Using 5,5 mm Ns and A, c/on 23(26) sts and work 8 cm in K1, P1 rib. Change to 8 mm Ns and cont in st st, inc 12 sts evenly across first row. [35(38) sts.] Cont by inc 1 st at each end of every 5th row 9 times. [53(56) sts.] When work measures 40(41) cm from beg, ending with a WS row, work 6 rows in B, then complete work in D. **At the same time,** when work measures 42(43) cm from beg, ending with a WS row **shape raglan:** c/off 3 sts at beg of next 2 rows, 2 sts at beg of next 2 rows, then dec 1 st each end of fol 15(16) rows until 13(14) sts rem, ending with a WS row. C/off 4 sts at beg and dec 1 st at end of next row. Work 1 row. Rep last 2 rows once. C/off rem 3(4) sts.

LEFT SLEEVE

Work as for right sleeve, rev shaping and using E instead of D for the top section.

TO MAKE UP

Join both front raglan seams and one back raglan seam.

NECK BORDER

Using 8 mm Ns and B, pick up and K approximately 58(62) sts evenly around neck and work 9 cm in st st then c/off. The st st will roll onto the RS of the work. Stitch the 2nd back raglan seam and neck border seam, rev seam for rolled section. Stitch side and sleeve seams.

Fair Isle roll-neck

MATERIALS
Pingouin Pidou (50 g balls); 6(7) balls Dark blue (A); 5(6) balls Light blue (B); 2 balls each of Red (C) and Fuchsia (D). One pair each 5,5 mm and 6,5 mm needles.

MEASUREMENTS
To fit bust 87(92-97) cm; actual all-round measurement 102(108) cm; length to shoulder 56(59) cm; sleeve seam 44(45) cm.

TENSION
12 sts and 16 rows = 10 cm over st st using 6,5 mm Ns.

STITCHES USED
Fair Isle stocking stitch: Work from the chart, making sure you twist the yarn on wrong side of work at each colour change.

BACK
Using 5,5 mm Ns and B, c/on 57(61) sts and work 8 cm in single rib.* Change to 6,5 mm Ns and cont in Fair Isle st st, inc 4 sts evenly across first row [61(65) sts]. When work measures 41(43) cm from beg, shape armholes: c/off 4 sts at the beg of next 2 rows, then 1 st at the beg of next 4(6) rows [45(47) sts rem]. When work measures 61(64) cm, shape shoulders and neck: c/off 4(5) sts at the beg of next 2 rows. Next row: c/off 4 sts at the beg of next row, then c/off centre 15 sts for neck on the same row, work to end of row. Cont on this side only. C/off 4 sts at the beg of next row. C/off 3 sts at the beg of next row (neck shaping). C/off 4 sts at the beg of next row. Complete other side to match, reversing all shapings.

FRONT
Begin as given for back to *. Change to 6,5 mm Ns and cont in Fair Isle st st, inc 4 sts evenly across first row [61(65) sts], and reversing the Fair Isle motifs as folls: 8(10) sts in B, 11 sts in D, 11 sts in C and 31(33) sts in A [on the 15th row work 19(21) sts in A, 11 sts in D, 11 sts in C, 20(22) sts in B].
When work measures 41(43) cm, shape armholes: work the same shapings at each end of work as given for back. When work measures 55(58) cm, shape neck: c/off centre 7 sts, then cont each side separately, c/off at neck edge on every alt row as folls: 2 sts (3 times) and 1 st (once). When work measures 61(64) cm, work the 3 shoulder shapings as given for back. Complete other side to match, reversing all shapings.

RIGHT SLEEVE
Using 5,5 mm Ns and A, c/on 24(26) sts and work 8 cm in single rib. Change to 6,5 mm Ns and cont in st st, inc 12 sts evenly across first row [36(38) sts on needle] and working as folls:* 14 rows in A, 14 rows in B* and inc 1 st at each end of every 8th row (6 times). [48(50) sts.]
When work measures approximately 41(43) cm from beg (at the same level on the section in B as for back and front), shape armholes; c/off 3 sts at the beg of next 2 rows, then 2 sts at the beg of next 2 rows, then 1 st at the beg of next 16(18) rows, then 2 sts at the beg of next 2 rows, then 5 sts at the beg of next 2 rows. C/off rem 8 sts.

LEFT SLEEVE
Using 5,5 mm Ns and A, c/on 24(26) sts and work 8 cm in single rib. Change to 6,5 mm Ns and cont in st st, working the same instructions as for the right sleeve, but working the following colour sequence: *14 rows in B, 14 rows in A*.

TO MAKE UP
Stitch right shoulder seam.

COLLAR
Using 6,5 mm Ns and A, pick up and knit 42 sts around front neck, then 25 sts across back neck. Work 27 cm in rev st st and c/off.
Stitch left shoulder seam and collar seam, rev the seam for the section of the collar to be turned over.
Stitch side seams.
Stitch sleeve seams. Sew in sleeves.
Illustrated on front cover.

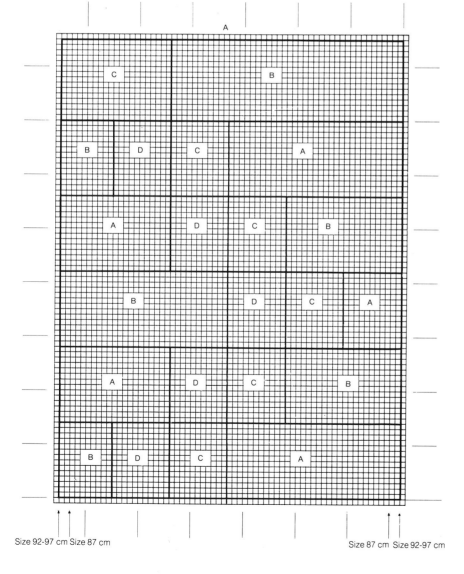

Size 92-97 cm Size 87 cm   Size 87 cm Size 92-97 cm

Wrapover jacket

MATERIALS
Orage (50 g balls); 17(18;19) balls; 1 pair 4,5 mm knitting needles; shoulder pads (optional).

MEASUREMENTS
To fit bust 81-87(92;97-102) cm; actual all round measurement (as worn) 113(119;124) cm; sleeve seam 36(38; 40) cm.

TENSION
22 sts and 22 rows = 10 cm using twist rib and 4,5 mm Ns.

STITCHES USED
Twist rib:
First row (right side): P1, * K1 tbl, P1; rep from * to end.
2nd row: K1 tbl, * P1, K1 tbl; rep from * to end.
These 2 rows form patt.

BACK
C/on 125(131;137) sts and work in patt as given above. Cont until work measures 33(34;35) cm from beg, ending with a 2nd patt row.

SHAPE ARMHOLES
C/off 2 sts at beg of next 6(6; 8) rows and 1 st at beg of next 12(14;12) rows. Cont on rem 101(105;109) sts until work measures 59(62;64) cm from beg, ending with WS row.

SHAPE SHOULDERS
C/off RW 11(11;12) sts at beg of next 4 rows and 10(11;11) sts at beg of next 2 rows. Cut yarn and leave rem 37(39;39) sts on a holder.

RIGHT FRONT
C/on 79(83;87) sts and work in patt; cont until work matches back to armhole but ending with a first patt row.

SHAPE ARMHOLE
C/off 2 sts at beg of next row and next 2(2;3) alt rows and 1 st at same edge on next 6(7;6) alt rows. Cont on rem 67(70;73) sts until work matches back to shoulder, ending at side edge.

SHAPE SHOULDER
C/off RW 11(11;12) sts at beg of next and fol alt row and 10(11;11) sts at same edge on next alt row **. Leave rem 35(37;38) sts on a holder without cutting yarn.

LEFT FRONT
Rev all shapings, work as for right front to ** thus ending at front edge after a RS row. Work 1 row on rem 35(37;38) sts then cut yarn and leave sts on a holder.

COLLAR
Return to sts of right front and with RS facing work 34(36;37) sts, then in correct rib work rem st tog with first st of back, work next 35(37;37) sts, work rem st tog with first st of left front, then work rem 34(36;37) sts. Cont on 105(111;113) sts and work in patt for 5 cm. C/off loosely RW.

SLEEVES
C/on 65(69;71) sts and work in patt but inc 1 st at both ends of every fol 4th row 3(4;5) times, then every alt row 31 times. Cont on 133(139;143) sts until work measures 36(38;40) cm from beg.

SHAPE TOP
C/off RW 5 sts at beg of next 12(6;2) rows and 6 sts at beg of next 10(16;20) rows. C/off rem 13 sts.

TO MAKE UP
Join shoulder seams matching rib. Sew in sleeves easing in fullness to fit, then join sleeve seams. Join side seams rev seam on 8 rows at lower edge. Turn up these rows onto RS and slip-stitch neatly in place. Sew in shoulder pads.

Saddle shoulder jacket

MATERIALS
Classic Confortable Sport (50 g balls); 15(16;17;17;18) balls. One pair each 4 mm, 4,5 mm and 5 mm knitting needles; 5 buttons.

MEASUREMENTS
To fit chest 97(102;107;112;117) cm.

TENSION
17 sts and 22 rows = 10 cm over st st using 5 mm Ns. Work a sample on 22 sts.

BACK
With 4,5 mm Ns c/on 89(93;97; 101;105) sts and work in rib.
First row (right side): P1, *K1, P1; rep from * to end.
2nd row: K1, * P1, K1; rep from * to end. Rep these 2 rows until work measures 5 cm ending with a 2nd row. Change to 5 mm Ns and work in st st. Cont without shaping until work measures 41(43;45; 46;47) cm from beg, ending with a P row.

ARMHOLE SHAPING
C/off 3(3;3;4;4) sts at beg of next 2 rows, 2 sts at beg of next 2(2;4;4;4) rows and 1 st at beg of next 6(8;6;6;8) rows. Cont on rem 73(75;77;79;81) sts until work measures 57(60;63;64;66) cm from beg, ending with a P row.

SHOULDER SHAPING
C/off 4(4;4;4;5) sts at beg of next 8 rows and 6(6;7;7;4) sts at beg of next 2 rows. C/off rem 29(31;31;33;33) sts for back neck.

POCKET LININGS
Make 2 alike. With 5 mm Ns c/on 25(25;25;27;27) sts and work in st st for 11(11;12;12;13) cm ending with a P row. Leave sts on a holder.

RIGHT FRONT
With 4,5 mm Ns c/on 45(47;49;51;53) sts and work in rib as on back welt for same number of rows. Change to 5 mm Ns and work in st st until work measures 16(16;17;17;18) cm from beg, ending with a P row.

POCKET OPENING
Next row: K15(15;17;17;19), slip off next 25(25;25;27;27) sts onto a holder, K sts of one pocket lining then K rem 5(7;7;7;7) sts at side edge. Cont in st st across all sts until work measures 37(39;41;42;43) cm from beg, ending at front edge.

FRONT SHAPING
Dec 1 st at beg of next row and next 4(4;2;5;3) alt rows then dec 1 st at same edge on every fol 3rd row 10(11;13;11;13) times. **At the same time** keep side edge straight until work matches back to armhole, ending at side.

ARMHOLE SHAPING
C/off 3(3;3;4;4) sts at beg of next row, 2 sts at same edge on next 2(2;3; 3;3) alt rows and 1 st on next 3(4;3;3;4) alt rows. Now keep this edge straight until work matches back to shoulder, ending at side edge.

SHOULDER SHAPING
C/off 5 sts at beg of next and fol 2 alt rows. Work 1 row then c/off rem 5(5; 6; 6; 7) sts.

LEFT FRONT
Work as for right front rev pocket opening and all shapings.

RIGHT SLEEVE
With 4,5 mm Ns c/on 49(51;55;57;59) sts and work in rib as on back welt until work measures 8 cm ending with a first row then rib 1 more row working 4 incs evenly spaced. [53(55;59;61;63) sts.] Change to 5 mm Ns and work in st st but inc 1 st at both ends of every fol 10th row 5(2;2;3;1) times, then every fol 8th row 3(7;7;6;9) times. Cont on 69(73;77;79;83) sts until work measures 47(48;48;49;50) cm from beg, ending with a P row.

TOP SHAPING
C/off 3(3;3;4;4) sts at beg of next 2 rows, 2 sts at beg of next 4(4;6;6;6) rows, 1 st at beg of next 12(14;14;14;16) rows, 2 sts at beg of next 2 rows and 4

sts at beg of next 6 rows. Cont on rem 15(17;17;17;19) sts for saddle yoke; work 11,5(11,5;12;12;13) cm without shaping, ending with a P row. C/off 5(5;5;5;6) sts at beg of next and fol alt row. Work 1 row then c/off the rem 5(7;7; 7;7) sts.

LEFT SLEEVE
Work as for right sleeve but at end of the saddle yoke work shapings at opposite edge.

POCKET BORDERS
Slip sts from holder at one pocket opening onto a 4,5 mm N and join on yarn with RS facing. K 1 row working 4 incs then cont on these 29(29; 29; 31; 31) sts and beg with 2nd row work in rib for 5 rows. C/off loosely RW. Work similar border on other pocket.

FRONT BORDER
With 4 mm Ns c/on 11 sts and work in rib.
First row (right side): K2, [P1, K1] 4 times, K1.
2nd row: [K1, P1] 5 times, K1. Rep these 2 rows 2(2;2;1;2) times then make buttonhole.
Next row: Rib 4, c/off 3, rib to end. On fol row c/on 3 sts over buttonhole. Cont in rib making 4 more buttonholes each 8(8,5; 9; 9,5; 9,5) cm above cast-off edge of previous one then cont until border, when slightly stretched, fits all round front, saddle yoke and neck edges of jacket. Leave sts on a safety pin with some yarn attached for adjustment.

TO MAKE UP
Sew in sleeves joining sides of saddle yokes to front and back shoulder edges. Join side and sleeve seams. Slip-st pocket linings in place on WS and neatly sew ends of borders on right side. Pin front border in place with buttonholes to left front and stretching border slightly around neck edges so that it fits well. Adjust length if necessary and cast off. Sew border in place as pinned and sew on buttons to correspond with buttonholes.

Lady's twin set

MATERIALS
Confort DK (50 g balls); **Pullover:** 5(5;5;6;6) balls; **Cardigan:** 6(7;8;8;9) balls; 1 pair each 3,25 mm and 4 mm knitting needles; 5 buttons.

MEASUREMENTS
To fit bust 92(97;102;107;112) cm; actual all round measurement 99(104,5; 110;114;119) cm; length to shoulder, **Pullover:** 54(54;55;55;56) cm; **Cardigan:** 55(55;56;56;57) cm; sleeve length 46(46;47;47;48) cm.

TENSION
22 sts and 26 rows = 10 cm over st st using 4 mm Ns.

Pullover

BACK
Using 3,25 mm Ns, c/on 109(115;121; 125;131) sts and work 5,5 cm K1, P1 rib. Change to 4 mm Ns * and cont in st st until work measures 32(32;32;31; 31) cm from beg, ending with a WS row. V.

SHAPE ARMHOLES
C/off 4(4;5;6;6) sts at beg of next 2 rows, 3(3;4;4;4) sts at beg of fol 2 rows, 2 sts at beg of next 2 rows and 1 st at beg of fol 10(12;14;14;16) rows. [81(85; 85;87;91) sts.] ** Cont straight until work measures 54(54;55;55;56) cm from beg, ending with a WS row.

SHAPE SHOULDERS AND NECK
C/off 6(7;7;7;7) sts at beg of next 4 rows.
Next row: C/off 7(7;7;7;8) sts, K until there are 11(11;11;12;13) sts on right N and leave these for right back, c/off 21 sts, K to end. Cont on 18(18;18;19;21) sts rem on N for left back. C/off 7(7;7;7;8) sts at beg of next row and 4 sts at neck edge at beg of fol row. C/off rem 7(7;7;8;8) sts. Rejoin yarn to neck edge of rem sts. C/off 4 sts, P to end then c/off rem 7(7;7;8;8) sts.

FRONT
Work as for back to *. Work 2 rows st st then beg patt panel as follows:
First row: K53(56;59;61;64), K2tog, yfd, K to end.
2nd and fol alt rows: P to end.
3rd row: K52(55;58;60;63), K2tog, yfd, K1, yfd, SKPO, K to end.
5th row: K51(54;57;59;62), K2tog, yfd, K3, yfd, SKPO, K to end.
7th row: K50(53;56;58;61), K2tog, yfd, K5, yfd, SKPO, K to end.
9th row: K52(55;58;60;63) yfd, SKPO, K1, K2tog, yfd, K to end.
11th row: K53(56;59;61;64), yfd, SKTPO, yfd, K to end.
12th row: P to end.
These 12 rows form patt panel. Keeping patt panel correct, cont as for back to **.
Cont straight until work measures 44(44;44;44;45) cm from beg, ending with a WS row.

SHAPE NECK AND SHOULDER
K35(37;37;38;40) sts, turn and leave rem sts on spare N for right front, c/off 3 sts at beg of next and fol alt row then 1 st at same edge on fol 3(3;3;3;4) alt rows. [26(28;28;29;30) sts.] Cont straight until work matches back to shoulder, ending with a WS row. C/off 6(7;7;7;7) sts at beg of this and next alt row, then 7(7;7;7;8) sts at beg of next alt row. C/off rem 7(7;7;8;8) sts. With RS facing, rejoin yarn to neck edge of rem sts, c/off 11 sts and complete to match first side, rev shaping.

NECKBAND

Stitch right shoulder seam. With RS facing, using 3,25 mm Ns, pick up and K90(90;96;98;104) sts evenly around neck edge. Work 3 cm K1, P1 rib. C/off loosely RW.

ARMBANDS

Stitch rem shoulder and neckband seam. With RS facing, pick up and K90(90;96;98;104) sts around armhole, work 2 cm K1, P1 rib, c/off RW.

TO MAKE UP

Stitch side and armband seams.

Cardigan

BACK

Using 3,25 mm Ns, c/on 109(115;121; 125;131) sts and work 6 cm K1, P1 rib. Change to 4 mm Ns and cont in st st until work measures 55(55;56;56; 57) cm from beg, ending with a WS row. V.

SHAPE SHOULDERS AND NECK

C/off 8(9;10;10;11) sts at beg of next 4 rows. C/off 9(9;10;10;11) sts, K until 14(15;15;17;17) sts on right hand N, turn, leave rem sts on a spare N. C/off 5 sts at beg of next row, P to end, c/off rem 9(10;10;11;11) sts. With RS facing, rejoin yarn to neck edge of rem sts, c/off 31(31;31;33;33) sts, K to end. C/off 9(9;10;10;11) sts at beg of next alt row. C/off 5 sts at beg of next row, K to end. C/off rem 9(10;10;11;11) sts.

RIGHT FRONT

Using 3,25 mm Ns, c/on 54(57;60;62;65) sts and work 6 cm K1, P1 rib. Change to 4 mm Ns and work 2 rows st st. Beg patt panel as follows:
First row: K6, K2 tog, yfd, K to end.
Cont in patt as now set until work measures 32 cm from beg, ending with a WS row.

SHAPE FRONT NECK

Patt 13, K2tog, (dec), K to end. Cont to dec in this position every 3rd row 20(20;20;21;21) times in all. [34(37;40; 41;44) sts.] When work matches back to shoulder work shoulder shapings: with WS facing c/off 8(9;10;10;11) sts at beg of next 2 alt rows. C/off 9(9;10; 10;11) sts at beg of next alt row. Work 1 row, then c/off rem 9(10;10;11;11) sts.

LEFT FRONT

Work as for right front, rev patt and shapings.

SLEEVES

Using 3,25 mm Ns, c/on 52(52;54;54;56) sts and work 8 cm K1, P1 rib. Change to 4 mm Ns and cont in st st inc 1 st each end of every fol 5th row 18(18;19; 19;20) times in all. [88(88;92;92;96) sts.] Cont straight until sleeve measures 46(46;47;47;48) cm from beg. V. C/off loosely.

FRONT BAND

Using 3,25 mm Ns, c/on 13 sts and work 2 cm K1, P1 rib.
Next row (buttonhole): Rib 5, c/off 3, rib to end.

Next row: Rib, c/on 3 sts over c/off sts. Work 4 more buttonholes 5 cm apart. Cont straight until band, when slightly stretched, fits up right front around neck and down left front. Leave sts on a safety pin.

TO MAKE UP

Stitch shoulder seams. Place a marker 20(20;21;21;22) cm down from each side of shoulder seams. Stitch sleeves into position between markers. Stitch side and sleeve seams. Stitch band into position, adjust length, c/off RW. Sew on buttons. DO NOT IRON.

Index